# Pac-Man: The First Animated TV Show Based Upon a Video Game

### By Mark Arnold

Books by the same author:

*The Best of The Harveyville Fun Times!*

*Created and Produced by Total TeleVision productions*

*If You're Cracked, You're Happy, Part Won and Part Too*

*Mark Arnold Picks on The Beatles*

*Frozen in Ice: The Story of Walt Disney Productions 1966-1985*

*Think Pink: The DePatie-Freleng Story*

*Pocket Full of Dennis the Menace*

*The Harvey Comics Companion*

*Long Title: Looking for the Good Times; Examining the Monkees' Songs (with Michael A. Ventrella)*

*Aaaaalllviiinnn: The Story of Ross Bagdasarian, Sr., Liberty Records, Format Films and The Alvin Show*

*Headquartered: A Timeline of The Monkees Solo Years (with Michael A. Ventrella)*

*The Comedy of Jack Davis*

*The Comedy of John Severin*

*The TTV Scrapbook (with Victoria Biggers)*

# Pac-Man: The First Animated TV Show Based Upon a Video Game

*By Mark Arnold*
*Bear Manor Media*

2022

*Pac-Man: The First Animated TV Show Based Upon a Video Game*

© 2022 Mark Arnold and Fun Ideas Productions.

All rights to the Pac-Man characters are trademarks of Bally/Midway Manufacturing Company in the Western Hemisphere and by Bandai Namco Limited in the rest of the world. All rights to the versions used by Hanna-Barbara are owned by Warner Bros. Animation.

All rights to all other characters represented in this book are owned by their respective copyright holders or are in the public domain.

The material used in this book is used for historical purposes and literary criticism and review and is used by permission and is used as Fair Use to be illustrative for the text contained herein. It is not designed to plagiarize or in any other way infringe on the copyright or in any other way infringe on the copyrights of any copyrighted materials contained herein.

The opinions contained within the interviews contained in this book are those of the person being interviewed and do not necessarily reflect the opinion of the author.

First printing.

All Rights Reserved.

Reproduction in whole or in part without the author's permission is strictly forbidden. Permission is granted to other publications or media to excerpt the contents contained herein for review purposes provided that the correct credit and copyright information is included for any materials reproduced.

For information, contact:
Ben Ohmart - benohmart@gmail.com
BearManor Media

Cover and chapter illustrations by Dean Rankine.

Typesetting and layout by DataSmith Solutions.

Published in the USA by BearManor Media.

Library of Congress Cataloging-in-Publication Data
Arnold, Mark.
Pac-man: The First Animated TV Show Based Upon a Video Game / by Mark Arnold.
Includes index.

ISBN - 978-1-62933-937-5

DEDICATED TO SCOTT SHAW! AND BEN OHMART
for recommending that I write this book. It was actually
more fun than I expected.

# Contents

| | |
|---|---|
| Introduction | 1 |
| A Brief History of Hanna-Barbera Productions | 3 |
| A Brief History of Arcade Video Games | 15 |
| A Brief History of Pac-Man | 21 |
| A Brief History of The Pac-Man Cartoon Show by Hanna-Barbera | 30 |
| Who's Who on The Pac-Man Cartoon Show | 39 |
| Pac-Man Episode Guide | 66 |
| Pac-Man Model Sheets | 96 |
| Pac-Man Postscripts | 121 |
| Index | 127 |

# Acknowledgements

Dean Rankine, Mark Evanier, Sergio Lehman. Apologies to anyone whom I have forgotten. Your contributions are noted.

# Introduction

Ok, I must admit that this book REALLY came out of left field. In the past, Ben Ohmart has suggested books that I could do and it's usually something to do with something I'm interested in like *Cracked* or *Mad*. This time, thanks to a quick recommendation by cartoonist Scott Shaw! on his Facebook page, I was suddenly drafted to write this book.

I have never expressed huge interest in video games and have said that a Hanna-Barbera book would be a massive undertaking if done correctly. In fact, for those wanting a good Hanna-Barbera history, I recommend five books: *The Art of Hanna-Barbera: Fifty Years of Creativity* by Ted Sennett, *Hanna-Barbera Cartoons* by Mike Mallory, *The Hanna-Barbera Treasury* by Jerry Beck, *A Cast of Friends* by William Hanna, and *My Life in Toons* by Joseph Barbera. At press time, there is a new book called *Hanna-Barbera: A History* by Jared Bahir Browsh. I haven't read it yet. It seems highly academic.

In any case, although I did occasionally watch the Hanna-Barbera *Pac-Man* cartoons since they were part of *The Pac-Man/Little Rascals/Richie Rich Show*, I figured I would take on the challenge. I was already watching due to me being a huge Harvey Comics and Richie Rich fan and a Little Rascals fan.

It turns out that a few of the cartoons are quite good and that I found myself actually laughing out loud at some of the episodes, particularly "Happy Pacs-giving", "Pac Van Winkle" and especially "Public Pac-Enemy No. 1" which I consider the best of the series. In fact, I consider the second season better than the first with the additions of P.J. and the dim-witted Super-Pac. It's a surprisingly funny show considering that Hanna-Barbera was really churning it out at the time.

Pac-Man was one of my favorite video games during that golden age and I will describe its origins later in this book. I was one of those people who would go to the video arcade for a few hours to try some new games, but also play some of my favorites like Asteroids, Dig Dug, Burger Time, Donkey Kong,

Tempest, Frogger, Centipede, Space Invaders, and of course, Pac-Man and Ms. Pac-Man.

In order to make this work, I decided to make this book short and fun. Usually, I write these big 700 page tomes that - as Stu Shostak of *Stu's Show* likes to say - make a better doorstop than a book. Well, forgive me, I just like to be thorough! I'm just as thorough here, but I decided to make it more streamlined and keep it under 100 pages. I'm even going to keep this Introduction short. I think I've succeeded.

—**Mark.**

# A Brief History of Hanna-Barbera Productions

Bill Hanna and Joe Barbera are iconic in the world of animation. Though some may disparage a large amount of their work, the fact that so many of their characters are memorable to this day 50 and 60 years after their original release is a testament to their creativity.

Hanna and Barbera first made their mark at MGM Studios in 1939 when they teamed up to make a number of cartoons featuring the cat and mouse team of Tom & Jerry. The first one called "Puss Gets the Boot" was released in 1940. They continued to make 114 Tom & Jerry cartoons until the animation studios were shut down in 1957. New cartoons were released through 1958. Over the years, the Tom & Jerry series won seven Academy Awards for Best Cartoon Short Subject. The series was also nominated for six additional Oscars.

The team ventured outside of MGM a little bit, most notably animating the stick figures of Lucille Ball and Desi Arnaz on the openings and closings of the original CBS network runs of *I Love Lucy* from 1951-1957.

Ironically, both MGM's animation studios and *I Love Lucy* came to an end in 1957 leaving Hanna and Barbera without work and without any solid future prospects. The decision was made for them to branch out and form their own company, and produce animation material exclusively for television. During their last year at MGM, Hanna and Barbera started developing the idea for what would become their first animated series and their own studio, *The Ruff and Reddy Show* which eventually debuted on NBC on December 14, 1957.

At first, they tried to talk MGM into the half hour show idea, but MGM weren't interested. Director George Sidney introduced Hanna and Barbera to the executives at Screen Gems television distribution, which was a division of rival movie studio Columbia Pictures, who had had recent success with the UPA line of animated shorts starring Mr. Magoo and Gerald McBoingboing.

Hanna-Barbara Enterprises was formed and they set up shop at the old Charlie Chaplin Studios on LaBrea Avenue in Hollywood. They were able to get the cream of the crop of animators due to the mass layoffs happening within the industry, so they recruited Michael Maltese, Warren Foster, Dan Gordon, Tony Benedict, Art Scott, Willie Ito, Kenneth Muse, Alex Love, Carlo Vinci and many others.

The *Ruff and Reddy* shorts took the same format of the first animated cartoons made for television, *Crusader Rabbit*. That is, short five minute cartoons serialized to make a longer story. The cartoons were designed to be shown individually as part of another show, or could be grouped together into a half-hour program. Namewise, the characters seem to be switched. The red cat is named Ruff and the dog, even though he has red hair on the top of his head is named Reddy. Unlike Tom & Jerry, Ruff and Reddy spoke a lot to compensate for the very limited animation, and they are best buddies instead of bitter enemies.

*The Ruff and Reddy Show* was very successful and lasted for three seasons, concluding its original run on April 2, 1960. In the meantime, Hanna-Barbera created another new series that was even more successful. It was called *The Huckleberry Hound Show* (1958-1961) starring a good-natured blue dog who spoke with a southern accent. Unlike *Ruff and Reddy*, *The Huckleberry Hound Show* had multiple five-minute segments that were also self-contained. The other segments included *Pixie and Dixie and Mr. Jinks* about a cat and two mice and *Yogi Bear* about an Ed Norton-like bear. The *Yogi Bear* segment was so successful, he got his own show in 1961 and he was replaced by *Hokey Wolf*, a conman wolf in the vein of *Sgt. Bilko*. *Huckleberry Hound* was very successful and originally ran through 1961. It was originally syndicated and sponsored by Kellogg's cereal. In April 1967, it was released from advertiser control and syndicated again.

For some reason, Hanna-Barbera still felt there was some viability to theatrical cartoons, so they created the French-Canadian wolf, *Loopy De Loop*, whose theatrical film series resembled a Hanna-Barbera TV show. The series lasted for

48 shorts from 1958-1965. The shorts were eventually aired on television in syndication in 1969.

Next up was *The Quick Draw McGraw Show* (1959-1961) which followed the same format as *Huckleberry Hound*. This time the star was a clumsy horse and his donkey sidekick named Baba Louie. The other segments were *Augie Doggie and Doggie Daddy* about father and son dachshunds and *Snooper and Blabber*, about a cat and mouse detective agency. Like *Huckleberry Hound*, it was syndicated and sponsored by Kellogg's.

The success of these three series led to Hanna-Barbara's first series on network, ABC, and in primetime, called *The Flintstones*. Prior to *The Simpsons*, it was the most successful animated TV series in primetime, lasting six seasons from 1960-1966. It starred caveman Fred Flintstone, his wife Wilma, their pet Dino, Fred's friend and neighbor Barney Rubble, Barney's wife Betty, and later additions of children Pebbles and Bamm-Bamm, the Hopparoo and the Great Gazoo. The original concept was similar to *The Honeymooners*.

The success of *The Flintstones* led to other primetime shows for Hanna-Barbera, all with middling success originally, but later became iconic in their canon. These were the *Sgt. Bilko*-like *Top Cat* (1961-1962, ABC); the futuristic Flintstones called *The Jetsons* (1962-1963, ABC); the adventurous and somewhat serious *Jonny Quest* (1964-1965, ABC), and the live-action and animation hybrid *The New Adventures of Huckleberry Finn* (1968-1969, NBC).

In the meantime, Hanna-Barbera kept turning out funny animal shows with *The Yogi Bear Show* (1961-1962, syndication), which had two new segments: pink lion *Snagglepuss* and petite duck with bulldog guardian *Yakky Doodle and Chopper*.

This was soon followed by *The Hanna-Barbera New Cartoon Series* with Ed Wynn-like *Wally Gator*, swordsman turtle and sheepdog *Touché Turtle and Dum Dum* and lion and hyena *Lippy the Lion and Hardy Har Har*. The show was also syndicated and originally ran during 1962-1963.

In 1963, with Hanna-Barbera expanding, they moved to the building most associated with Hanna-Barbera at 3400 Cahuenga in Hollywood. The studio remained in this building until 1998. Shortly after this, Hanna-Barbera Records premiered. The label lasted into 1967 and was mainly an avenue to release albums featuring their various characters in many song and story albums, but they did release a few things by Les Baxter, Louis Prima and future Three Dog Night frontman Danny Hutton, who also ran the label.

This series in turn was followed by *The Magilla Gorilla Show* (1963-1967, syndicated and sponsored by Ideal toys), about an unsold gorilla in a pet shop. The other segments were a sheriff and deputy named *Ricochet Rabbit and Droop-a-Long*, and yet another cat and mouse in a country setting called *Punkin' Puss and Mushmouse*.

This was followed by *The Peter Potamus Show* (1964-1966, syndicated and sponsored by Ideal toys) starring a hippopotamus who traveled in a hot air balloon with a monkey. The show also contained the polar bear and seal named

*Breezly and Sneezly* and the three canine Musketeers named *Yippee, Yappee and Yahooey*.

On June 3, 1964, Hanna-Barbera released their first animated theatrical feature film called *Hey There, It's Yogi Bear*. The film was successful and was followed up on August 3, 1966 by *The Man Called Flintstone*. Though not as successful, both films also had a successful life on television. Hanna-Barbera would not do another animated theatrical feature film until 1973. Fred and Barney also made a cameo appearance in the 1966 animated primetime special about *Alice in Wonderland or What's a Nice Girl Like You Doing in a Place Like This?*

That same year, the live-action sitcom *Bewitched* debuted on ABC-TV. Like they had done years ago for *I Love Lucy*, Hanna-Barbera created animated titles for the series. The series lasted until 1972, and Darrin and Samantha from the show appeared on an episode of *The Flintstones* in animated form.

This was followed by the first Hanna-Barbera TV show especially created for Saturday mornings: The hour-long *Atom Ant/Secret Squirrel Show* that ran from 1965-1968 on NBC. Eventually the hour-long show was broken up into two half-hours. Superhero Atom Ant also featured an old grandmother and her dog called *Precious Pupp*, and there was the self-descriptive *Hillbilly Bears*. Spy Secret Squirrel had a purple squid named *Squiddly Diddly* and a friendly, but inept witch named *Winsome Witch*.

Next, Hanna-Barbera went back to syndication and this time teamed up with American International Pictures for the *Sinbad Jr. and his Magic Belt* series (1965-1966).

The following syndicated show was done in conjunction with Larry Harmon Productions and Wolper Productions who produced an animated version of the classic *Laurel and Hardy* comedy team. Both original comedians had passed by the time this show aired during 1966-1967, so Larry Harmon and Jim MacGeorge provided the voices of the famous duo.

The next year, Hanna-Barbera took on Abbott and Costello with the syndicated *Abbott and Costello Cartoon Show*, which aired during 1967-1968. It was a joint venture with RKO General and Jomar Productions. This time, Bud Abbott provided his own voice, while Stan Irwin portrayed the voice of the late Lou Costello.

Another syndicated series was called *The Space Kidettes* (1966-1967). Originally, due to being sponsored by General Mills, episodes were paired with Total TeleVision's *Tennessee Tuxedo* or *Go Go Gophers*. Later, episodes were paired up with Hanna-Barbera's *Young Sampson* (originally called *Sampson and Goliath*), about a boy and his lion.

It was around this time that Hanna-Barbara was sold to Taft Broadcasting. The studio originally went up for sale in 1965, but due to lawsuits preventing the sale by Columbia Pictures, the sale didn't go through for at least another year completing the sale in October 1966. H-B Veteran Tony Benedict confirms that the Golden Age of Hanna-Barbera ended that day.

From this point on through the end of Hanna-Barbera, the majority of Hanna-Barbera series were done for Saturday morning on the networks (ABC, CBS and NBC) or for syndication. *Frankenstein Jr. and The Impossibles* was one of the network shows, featuring a robot Frankenstein's monster and a trio of superheroes in their separate cartoon adventures. The show aired on CBS from 1966-1968.

Superheroes were now the order of the day, Gone were the funny animal characters at Hanna-Barbera for about two years. In quick succession, Hanna-Barbera did *Space Ghost and Dino Boy* (1966-1968, CBS); *Birdman and the Galaxy Trio* (1967-1969, NBC); *The Herculoids* (1967-1968, CBS); *Shazzan* (1967-1969, CBS); *The Fantastic Four* (1967-1970, ABC) based upon the Marvel Comics comic book series; *Moby Dick and Mighty Mightor* (1967-1969, CBS); and *The Adventures of Gulliver* (1968-1969, ABC). All of these shows were later repackaged for syndication as *Hanna-Barbera's World of Super Adventure*, and aired from 1980-1984.

New episodes of *Space Ghost* and of *The Herculoids* were later made as part of the *Space Stars* series (1981-1982, NBC). This series also had additional segments of *Teen Force, Astro and the Space Mutts* and the *Space Stars Finale*, where all of the characters from all of the segments teamed up.

So many superhero and action adventure shows on Saturday morning TV caused public outcry by a group called ACT or Action for Children's Television. They claimed there was too much violence on Saturday morning TV, so Hanna-Barbera responded by returning to more comical TV shows rather than the serious action adventure shows.

The first new show out of the gate was Hanna-Barbera's first major foray into live-action. There was live-action in a Gene Kelly special called *Jack and the Beanstalk* that aired on February 26, 1967, but this is the first regular series to feature it called *The Banana Splits Adventure Hour* (1968-1970, NBC), sponsored by Kellogg's. The show featured many segments including *Arabian Knights, The Three Musketeers, Micro Ventures* and the live-action *Danger Island*, directed by a young Richard Donner, who would go on to direct 1978's *Superman: The Movie*. *The Banana Splits* spawned a hit album and a few hit singles.

The next comedy series was *The Wacky Races* (1968-1970, CBS), a show made in conjunction with Heatter-Quigley Productions, the company best known for producing *The Hollywood Squares*. *Wacky Races* also was originally supposed to be a game show. The show spun off two series: *The Perils of Penelope Pitstop* (1969-1971, CBS) and *Dastardly and Muttley in Their Flying Machines* (1969-1971, CBS).

*The Cattanooga Cats* (1969-1971, ABC) was an attempt to recapture The Banana Splits' success, but it was only moderately so. They had an album, they had a single, they had other segments (*Around the World in 79 Days, It's the Wolf, Motormouse and Autocat*), but it wasn't remotely as successful. Perhaps because it was fully animated instead of live-action.

Hanna-Barbera ended the decade with what would become their signature production, eclipsing even *The Flintstones*, *Yogi Bear* and *Huckleberry Hound*. It was *Scooby-Doo, Where Are You?* (1969-1971, CBS and 1978-1979, ABC). The show was the template for so many Hanna-Barbera shows of the 1970s, making the studio quite a cookie cutter one from this point forward.

As the 70s began, there was a brief return to primetime with *Where's Huddles?* Although basically a retread of *The Flintstones* in modern times as a football team, the show only lasted 10 episodes on CBS as a summer replacement series. They would have better luck with *Wait Till Your Father Gets Home*, which ran from 1972-1974 in syndication, after an animated pilot that appeared on *Love, American Style*.

Hanna-Barbera contributed to the *Famous Classic Tales* series (1970-1984, CBS), although most of their contributions appeared from 1973-1981. They were animated by Hanna-Barbera's Australian division and included *The Count of Monte Cristo*, *20,000 Leagues Under the Sea*, *The Three Musketeers*, *The Last of the Mohicans*, *Davy Crockett on the Mississippi*, *Five Weeks in a Balloon*, *Black Beauty*, *Gulliver's Travels* and *Daniel Boone*.

Hanna-Barbara continued with the format started with The Banana Splits of a pop music LP tied into their TV series. This was done for *Harlem Globetrotters* (1970-1973, 1978, CBS) and *Josie and the Pussycats* (1970-1972, CBS). Both series' LPs flopped, but both TV shows warranted sequel series: *The Super Globetrotters* (1979-1980, NBC) and *Josie and the Pussycats in Outer Space* (1972-1974, CBS). All four series were licensed properties, a phenomenon that would increase with Hanna-Barbara in subsequent years, as fewer home-grown properties would be created by the company. The *Josie* shows were an attempt to replicate the success of the various Archie shows animated by Filmation, as Josie was also an Archie Comics character.

Hanna-Barbera also tried to replicate the success of their own properties throughout the 1970s with spin-offs of *The Flintstones* called *The Pebbles and Bamm-Bamm Show* (1971-1972, CBS); *The Flintstone Comedy Hour* (1972-1974, CBS); *Fred Flintstone and Friends* (1977-1978, syndicated); *Captain Caveman and the Teen Angels* (1977-1980, ABC); *The New Fred and Barney Show* (1979, NBC); *Fred and Barney Meet the Thing* (featuring The Thing from *The Fantastic Four*) (1979, NBC); *Fred and Barney Meet the Shmoo* (featuring the Shmoo from *Li'l Abner* (1979-1980, NBC); *The Flintstone Comedy Show* (1980-1982, NBC); *The Flintstone Funnies* (1982-1984, NBC); *The Flintstone Kids* (1986-1988, ABC), plus a dozen or more primetime *Flintstones* specials produced from 1977-1994.

Also, there was *The Flintstones*, then *The Jetsons*, why not split the difference with *The Roman Holidays* (1972-1973, NBC)? Then there was *Yogi Bear*, so why not *Help! It's the Hair Bear Bunch* (1971-1972, CBS)? Next there was *Jonny Quest*, why not *Sealab 2020* (1972-1973, NBC)? These were the days of derivative shows for Hanna-Barbera.

Speaking of Yogi Bear, new series featuring your average bear included: *Yogi's Gang* (1973-1974, ABC); *Yogi's Space Race* (1978-1979, NBC) which also featured segments *Galaxy Goof-Ups* and *Buford and the Galloping Ghost*; *Yogi's Treasure Hunt* (1985-1988, syndication); *The New Yogi Bear Show* (1988, syndication); and *Yo Yogi!* (1991-1993, NBC, syndication).

*Yogi's Gang* actually began as a movie called *Yogi's Ark Lark* made for *The ABC Saturday Superstar Movie* (1972-1974, ABC), a movie series with rare cooperation by all the major American animation studios at the time. Hanna-Barbera contributed seven movies to this series, while the others were contributed by Filmation, Rankin/Bass, DePatie-Freleng, Hal Seeger Productions and Fred Calvert Productions.

Besides *Yogi's Ark Lark*, the Hanna-Barbera films were *Oliver and the Artful Dodger*, *The Adventures of Robin Hoodnik*, *Gidget Makes the Wrong Connection*, *The Banana Splits in Hocus Pocus Park*, *Tabitha and Adam and the Clown Family* and from season two, *Lost in Space*.

Speaking of movies, the time was right for Hanna-Barbera to release another theatrical feature film. This time it was *Charlotte's Web* in 1973 and they took the Disney route by offering fuller animation and even threw in the Sherman Brothers who wrote music for numerous Disney films for good measure. Next was *Baxter!*, also from 1973 and *C.H.O.M.P.S.* from 1979, both live-action. Then back to animation again for *Heidi's Song* (1982); *GoBots: Battle of the Rock Lords* (1986); *Ultraman: The Adventure Begins* (1987); *Jetsons: The Movie* (1990); *Once Upon a Forest* (1993); and the live-action *The Flintstones* (1994) and *The Flintstones in Viva Rock Vegas* (2000). The Hanna-Barbera feature division was spun into Turner Feature Animation.

Hanna-Barbera and some of these other studios also contributed to *The ABC Afterschool Special* series (1972-1997, ABC), though the majority of H-B's contributions were live-action. They included *The Last of the Curlews*, *Cyrano*, *The Runaways*, *The Crazy Comedy Concert*, *It Isn't Easy Being a Teenage Millionaire* and *The Gymnast*.

Hanna-Barbera also tried to replicate the success of *Scooby-Doo* with not only a number of spin-off shows, but also a number of rip-off shows. These included *The New Scooby-Doo Movies* (1972-1974, CBS); *The Scooby-Doo/Dynomutt Hour* (1976-1977, ABC); *Scooby's All-Starr Laff-a-Lympics* (1977-1979, ABC); *Scooby-Doo and Scrappy-Doo* (1979-1980, ABC); *The Richie Rich/Scooby-Doo Show* (1980-1982, ABC); *The Scooby & Scrappy-Doo/Puppy Hour* (*Puppy's New Adventures* by Ruby-Spears) (1982-1983, ABC); *The New Scooby and Scrappy-Doo Show* (1983-1984, ABC); *Scary Scooby Funnies* (1984-1985, ABC); *The 13 Ghosts of Scooby-Doo* (1985, ABC); *Scooby's Mystery Funhouse* (1985-1986, ABC); *The Funky Phantom* (1971-1972, ABC); *The Amazing Chan and the Chan Clan* (1972-1973, CBS); *Speed Buggy* (1972-1973, CBS); *Butch Cassidy and the Sundance Kids* (1973-1974, NBC); *Goober and the Ghost Chasers* (1973-1975, ABC); *Clue Club* (1976-1977, CBS); and *Jabberjaw* (1976-1978, ABC).

Another development during the 1970s and 1980s was to make Saturday morning animated versions of live-action primetime shows, sometimes directly with most or all of the actual voice talent, or inspired by. These included: *Inch High, Private Eye* (*Get Smart*) (1973-1974, NBC); *Jeannie* (*I Dream of Jeannie*) (1973-1975, CBS); *The Addams Family* (1973-1975, NBC); *Hong Kong Phooey* (*Kung Fu*) (1973-1975, ABC); *Devlin* (Evil Knievel) (1974-1975, ABC); *Partridge Family 2200 A.D.* (*The Partridge Family*) (1974-1975, CBS); *These Are the Days* (*The Waltons*) (1974-1975, ABC); and *Valley of the Dinosaurs* (*Land of the Lost*) (1974-1976, CBS); *The Fonz and the Happy Days Gang* (*Happy Days*) (1980-1981, ABC); *Laverne & Shirley in the Army* (*Laverne & Shirley*) (1981-1982, ABC); *Mork & Mindy/Laverne & Shirley/Fonz Hour* (*Mork* segment by Ruby-Spears) (1982-1983, ABC); *The Gary Coleman Show* (*Diff'rent Strokes*) (1982-1983, NBC); and *The Dukes* (*The Dukes of Hazzard*) (1983-1984, CBS). *The Addams Family* would return years later with a reboot based upon the TV series and the feature film revival. It ran from 1992-1993 on ABC.

Hanna-Barbera teamed up with Eric Porter Studios and with Air Programs International in order to take on the added commitments and production orders.

Along with multiple *Flintstones*, *Scooby-Doo* and *Yogi Bear* shows, the big hit series for the rest of the 1970s and 1980s was *Super Friends* (1973-1974, ABC); *The All-New Super Friends Hour* (1977-1978, ABC); *Challenge of the Super Friends* (1978-1979, ABC); *The World's Greatest Super Friends* (1979-1980, ABC); *Super Friends* (1980-1982, ABC); *Super Friends: The Legendary Super Powers Show* (1984-1985, ABC); *The Super Powers Team: Galactic Guardians* (1985-1986, ABC). These were much, much less violent versions of the superheroes that Filmation did in the 1960s.

Occasionally, throughout all of this, Hanna-Barbera tried to come up with some original concepts, usually based upon the latest fads of the day. Examples included *Wheelie and the Chopper Bunch* (1974-1975, NBC); *The CB Bears* (1977-1978, NBC) which included the separate segments of *Posse Impossible*, *Blast-Off Buzzard*, *Undercover Elephant*, *Shake, Rattle and Roll*, and *Heyyy, It's the King!*; the live-action *Skatebirds* (1977-1978, CBS), an attempt to replicate *The Banana Splits* with animated segments of *Woofer and Wimper* (re-edited segments from *Clue Club*), *The Robonic Stooges*, *Wonder Wheels* and the live-action *Mystery Island*.

Hanna-Barbera also explored live-action again with *Korg: 70,000 B.C.* (1974-1976, ABC) as competitor Filmation was starting to make inroads into this same area.

After years of success, Hanna-Barbera decided to throw their former employers a bone and release *The Tom & Jerry/Grape Ape Show* (1975-1976, ABC), although Tom & Jerry were distinctly sanitized and non-violent in this series. In fact, they were friends. The only similarity to Tom & Jerry of old was that they remained mute. Like many Hanna-Barbera series of the 1970s, this series went through a number of incarnations: *The Tom & Jerry/Grape Ape/Mumbly Show* (1976, ABC); and *The Tom & Jerry/Mumbly Show* (1976-1977,

ABC). Mumbly was basically Muttley from the old *Wacky Races* series and was probably renamed to avoid paying royalties to Heatter-Quigley Productions. All three shows also appeared separately in syndication. Tom & Jerry returned years later in *Tom & Jerry Kids* (1990-1994, FOX); and its spin-off *Droopy, Master Detective* (with *Screwball Squirrel*) (1993-1994, FOX).

After this series, Hanna-Barbera tried to revive other dormant theatrical cartoon series. They succeeded with *The All New Popeye Hour* (1978-1983, CBS). This series also had a *Dinky Dog* segment. It was followed up by *Popeye and Son* (1987-1988, CBS). There were also two primetime Popeye specials.

*Dinky Dog* and *Drak Pack* (1980-1982, NBC) were both animated by Southern Star, Hanna-Barbera's Australian studio. Later Southern Star series included *The Berenstain Bears* (1985-1987, CBS); *CBS Storybreak* (1985-1987, CBS); and *Teen Wolf* (1986-1989, CBS).

Another dormant character was Casper the Friendly Ghost, so Hanna-Barbera came up with *Casper and the Angels* (1979-1980, NBC). The series also had two primetime specials. Harvey Comics owned Casper at this point and the next year they launched a show featuring their character named Richie Rich, but *Richie Rich* was never a standalone show. After launching as part of the aforementioned *Richie Rich/Scooby-Doo Show*, it was then renamed *The Pac-Man/Little Rascals/Richie Rich Show* (1982-1983, ABC) and then *The Monchichis/Little Rascals/Richie Rich Show* (1983-1984, ABC). *Pac-Man* was the very first animated series based upon a video game; *Little Rascals* was an animated version of the *Our Gang* shorts and *Monchichis* was yet another set of characters in the style of *The Smurfs*. *Richie Rich* was eventually recycled as part of *The Funtastic World of Hanna-Barbera* syndicated series.

*Pac-Man* proved to be so popular that the next year it was rechristened *The Pac-Man/Rubik, the Amazing Cube Hour* (1983-1984, ABC). *Rubik* was a Ruby-Spears production. There were also two *Pac-Man* holiday specials.

Yet another dormant character was Al Capp's Shmoo from the *Li'l Abner* comic strip. *The New Shmoo* aired during 1979 on NBC and then teamed up with Fred and Barney as mentioned earlier.

Hanna-Barbera tried once again to break back into primetime, this time with *The Hanna-Barbera Happy Hour* (1978, NBC) and with *Jokebook* (1982, NBC). Both were short-lived.

Through a strange transaction, Hanna-Barbara swapped proposed TV shows with DePatie-Freleng. Hanna-Barbara was scheduled to do another animated version of *The Fantastic Four*, while rival DFE was supposed to do an animated Godzilla series. H-B ended up doing *The Godzilla Power Hour* (1978-1981, NBC) and had great success. *Jana of the Jungle* was a segment of the show.

Later, Hanna-Barbera picked up on DePatie-Freleng's star character after DFE shut their doors and became Marvel Productions and issued *Pink Panther and Sons* (1984-1986, NBC-ABC).

As the decade of the 1970s closed, Hanna-Barbera produced an animated show starring the Mexican movie star Cantinflas called *Amigo and Friends* for the Latin American market. It ran from 1979-1982 through Televisa. Later, Hanna-Barbera did the same for France and issued *Lucky Luke* (1984-1985) based upon that graphic novel series.

During the years that Bill Hanna and Joseph Barbera worked for MGM, their prime rival making cartoons for the studio was Tex Avery. Avery left MGM like Hanna and Barbera did and briefly worked for Walter Lantz and then entered the world of advertising. In the twilight years of his life, he came back and worked for his old rivals, creating his final project before his death, *The Kwicky Koala Show* (1981-1982, CBS) with segments of *The Bungle Brothers*, *Crazy Claws* and *Dirty Dawg*.

Desperate for another long-lasting hit a la *Scooby-Doo*, Hanna-Barbera hit paydirt with *The Smurfs* (1981-1989, NBC), which spawned a number of home-grown and licensed imitations of little groups of characters, plus a half dozen primetime TV specials: *Trollkins* (1981-1982, CBS); *Shirt Tales* (1982-1984, NBC); the aforementioned *Monchichis*; *The Biskitts* (1983-1984, CBS); *Snorks* (1984-1989, NBC); *Paw Paws* (1985-1986, syndication); *Pound Puppies* (1986-1987, ABC); and *Foofur* (1986-1988, NBC).

As the 1980s wore on, a few more live-action series were created including *Benji, Zax & the Alien Prince* (1983-1984, CBS); and *Going Bananas* (1984-1985, NBC). There were also a number of live-action specials made by the studio that most didn't realize were made by Hanna-Barbera: *Hardcase* (1972); *Shootout in a One-Dog Town* (1974); *The Phantom Rebel* (1976); *The Gathering* (1977); *The Beasts are in the Streets* (1978); *KISS Meets the Phantom of the Park* (1978); *Legends of the Superheroes* (1979); *The Gathering, Part 2* (1979); *Belle Starr* (1980); *The Great Gilly Hopkins* (1981); *Deadline* (1982); *Return to Eden* (1983); *Shark's Paradise* (1986); *The Last Frontier* (1986); and *Stone Fox* (1987).

Like *The ABC Afterschool Specials*, Hanna-Barbara also contributed to the *ABC Weekend Specials* (1977-1997). Most of their contributions aired from 1983-1985 and one in 1992. They were *The Secret World of Og*, Part 1-3; *The Amazing Bunjee Venture*, Part 1-2; *The Return of the Bunjee*, Part 1-2; *The Velveteen Rabbit*; and *Monster in My Pocket: The Big Scream*.

Transforming robots became the rage in the mid-1980s, and while rival studio Marvel Productions got *The Transformers*, Hanna-Barbera got *Challenge of the GoBots* (1984-1985, syndication).

Also debuting in syndication was *The Funtastic World of Hanna-Barbera* (1985-1994) that featured both new and repeat shows. The series started initially with *Paw Paws* (1985-1987); *Galtar and the Golden Lance* (1985-1987); *HBTV* (1985-1987); *The Jetsons* (1985-1987; 1993-1994); and *Yogi's Treasure Hunt* (1985-1988). Changes were made every season so new shows were added as older shows were dropped. These were: *The New Adventures of Jonny Quest* (1986-1988); *Hanna-Barbera Superstars 10* (1987-1988); *Sky Commanders* (1987-1988); *Snorks* (1987-1989); *The Smurfs* (1987-1990); *Richie Rich* (1988-1989); *Skedaddle* (1988-1989); *The New Yogi Bear Show* (1988-1989); *The Flintstone Kids* (1988-1990); *The Further Adventures of SuperTed* (1988-1990);

*Fantastic Max* (1988-1990); *A Pup Named Scooby-Doo* (1988-1991); *Dink the Little Dinosaur* (a Ruby-Spears production) (1989-1991); *Paddington Bear* (1989-1991); *Bill and Ted's Excellent Adventures* (1990-1991); *The Adventures of Don Coyote and Sancho Panda* (1990-1992); *Wake, Rattle, and Roll* (1990-1992); *Midnight Patrol: Adventures in the Dream Zone* (1990-1993); *Young Robin Hood* (1991-1993); *The Pirates of Dark Water* (1992-1993); *Yo Yogi!* (1992-1993); *2 Stupid Dogs* (with *Super Secret Secret Squirrel*) (1993-1994); and *SWAT Kats: The Radical Squadron* (1993-1994).

The Hanna-Barbera Superstars 10 from The Funtastic World were this series of all-new fully-animated made-for-TV movies featuring classic Hanna-Barbera characters. The titles included *Yogi's Great Escape*; *The Jetsons Meet the Flintstones*; *Scooby-Doo Meets the Boo Brothers*; *Yogi Bear and the Magical Flight of the Spruce Goose*; *Top Cat and the Beverly Hills Cats*; *Scooby-Doo and the Ghoul School*; *Rockin' with Judy Jetson*; *The Good, the Bad and Huckleberry Hound*; *Yogi and the Invasion of the Space Bears*; and *Scooby-Doo and the Reluctant Werewolf*.

From 1985-1992, Hanna-Barbera also released *The Greatest Adventure: Stories from the Bible*, a 13-episode made-for-video animated film series.

*Wildfire* (1986-1987, CBS) was a latter-day attempt at the action-adventure genre.

Taft Broadcasting was bought out in a hostile takeover in April 1987 and the company was renamed Great American Broadcasting and Great American Communications. They were now the owners of both Hanna-Barbera and Ruby-Spears as Taft snapped up Ruby-Spears in 1981.

Comedian Martin Short from *SCTV* and *Saturday Night Live* created a live-action/animated series called *The Completely Mental Misadventures of Ed Grimley* (1988-1989, NBC). Fellow *SCTV* alum Joe Flaherty also appeared in live-action segments reprising his Count Floyd character. Another fellow SCTV alum, Rick Moranis, followed this show with his own *Gravedale High* (1990-1991, NBC).

The feature films of Bill and Ted spawned the animated series of *Bill and Ted's Excellent Adventures* (1990-1991, CBS). Keanu Reeves, Alex Winter, George Carlin and Bernie Casey reprised their film roles. Also, the feature films of *Dumb and Dumber* begat the similarly titled animated series that ran from 1995-1996 on ABC.

Hanna-Barbera also produced eight *Timeless Tales from Hallmark*: *Rapunzel*, *The Emperor's New Clothes*, *Thumbelina*, *The Ugly Duckling*, *The Elves and the Shoemaker*, *Rumpelstiltskin*, *Puss in Boots* and *The Steadfast Tin Soldier*.

Hanna-Barbera took over for DIC and their series *Captain Planet and the Planeteers* and produced *The New Adventures of Captain Planet* (1993-1996, TBS, syndication).

Over the years, there were also many unrealized projects for Hanna-Barbera. Some of them include *The World: Color it Happy* (1967, unsold pilot); *Taggart's Treasure* (1976, unsold live-action pilot); *The Beach Girls* (1977, unsold live-action pilot starring Rita Wilson); *The Funny World of Fred and Bunni* (1978, unsold live-action/animated primetime variety series starring Fred Travalena); *Sergeant T.K. Yu* (1979, unsold live-action TV crime drama series starring Johnny Yune); *America vs. the World* (1979, unsold live-action TV series hosted by Ed McMahon and Georgia Engel); and *The B.B. Beegle Show* (1980, unsold live-action/puppet TV series with Joyce DeWitt and Arte Johnson).

There were also random specials made over the years featuring holiday themes with no central Hanna-Barbera characters and specials that had no succeeding series. These included *A Christmas Story* (1972); *Silent Night, Holy Night* (1976); *The Harlem Globetrotters Meet Snow White* (1980); *Star Fairies* (1985); *Rock Odyssey* (1987); *The Little Troll Prince* (1987); *Hagar the Horrible: Hagar Knows Best* (1989); *The Yum Yums: The Day Things Went Sour* (1990); *The Last Halloween* (1991); *The Halloween Tree* (1993); *Jonny's Golden Quest* (1993); *The Town Santa Forgot* (1993); *Yogi the Easter Bear* (1994); *Daisy-Head Mayzie* (1995); and more.

As the 1990s began, *The Simpsons* was all the rage in primetime, so Hanna-Barbera followed up with *Fish Police* (1992, CBS) and *Capitol Critters* (1992, ABC).

Also, in 1991, Ted Turner acquired the Hanna-Barbera and Ruby-Spears libraries (as well as Hanna-Barbera's old stomping grounds of MGM) and it was all owned by Turner Broadcasting System. Then on October 1, 1992, Turner launched Cartoon Network, which originally aired virtually all of the original Hanna-Barbera library and later produced all-new shows including *What a Cartoon!* (1995-1997); *Dexter's Laboratory* (1997-1999); *The Real Adventures of Jonny Quest* (1996-1997); *Cave Kids* (1996); *Johnny Bravo* (1997-2002); *Cow and Chicken* (1997-1999); *I Am Weasel* (1997-2000); and *The Powerpuff Girls* (1998-2002).

Boomerang launched in 2000 and many of the older Hanna-Barbera shows that used to be on Cartoon Network moved to that channel.

By 2001, Hanna-Barbara was no more. Everything went under the umbrella of Warner Bros. Animation and Time Warner; however new series and films featuring Hanna-Barbera characters continued. Shows over the years included *Space Ghost Coast to Coast* (1994-1999); *Cartoon Planet* (1995-1998; 2012-2014); *The Brak Show* (2000-2003; 2007); *Aqua Teen Hunger Force* (2000-2015); *Sealab 2021* (2000-2005); *Harvey Birdman, Attorney at Law* (2000-2007; 2018); and others.

There are still movies being made today such as *Tom & Jerry: The Movie* (1992); the live-action *Scooby-Doo* (2002) and *Scooby-Doo 2: Monsters Unleashed* (2004); the live-action/animated *Yogi Bear* (2010); *Top Cat: The Movie* (2011); *Top Cat Begins* (2015); *Tom & Jerry: Spy Quest* (2015); *Daphne & Velma* (2018); the live-action *Banana Splits Movie* done as a horror film (2019); *Scoob!* (2020); *Tom & Jerry* (2021); *Jellystone!* (soon); and about a bazillion *Scooby-Doo* movies.

Bill Hanna passed away at the age of 90 on March 22, 2001.

Joseph Barbera passed away at the age of 95 on December 18, 2006.

# A Brief History of Arcade Video Games

The golden age of video games is considered to be between the years of 1971 and 1983 according to The History of Computing Project. The year 1971 was chosen as the earlier start date as it was the year that the creator of Pong, Allan Alcorn, filed a pivotal patent regarding video game technology. Pong was a table tennis-themed video arcade game from Atari featuring two white rectangles as paddles and a white square as the ball with large white numbers up top to keep score. Though considered tremendously simplistic today, it was the height of technology when the arcade game was released in 1972.

Pong was preceded by the very first video arcade game called Computer Space from 1971, which in turn was derivative of the 1962 computer game called Spacewar!, which was a game originally designed in the context of academic computer and programming research in demonstrations of computing power as computers started to get smaller and faster. Spacewar! and Computer Space were both the inspirations for the later game Asteroids, which was introduced in 1979.

After Pong became successful, Atari co-founder Ted Dabney (1937-2018) left in March 1973 as he felt overshadowed by his partner Nolan Bushnell and Ampex's Al Alcorn, who had come to Atari to help create Pong. Dabney had created the coin slot mechanism before his departure.

Atari and Kee Games were the arcade game leaders at this time and after Pong was a hit, many games were turned out by both companies from 1973-1978 in short order. In 1973, Kee had Elimination while Atari had Quadropong. In 1974, Kee had Spike, Formula K and Twin Racer while Atari had Rebound, Gran Trak 10 and Gran Trak 20, respectively.

Atari and Kee merged in November 1974 and produced Tank. Pursuit, Indy 800 and Tank II followed in 1975. Quiz Show, Tank 8, Indy 4 and Sprint 2 followed in 1976. Drag Race and Superbug came next in 1977 and Sprint 1 and Ultra Tank in 1978 after which Kee was shut down by Warner Communications, which had acquired Atari in 1976.

As an aside, one Atari employee who had helped to create a circuit board for Breakout in 1972, as a follow up to Pong, eventually teamed up with Steve Wozniak to form Apple Computers in 1976. His name was Steve Jobs, and it was Wozniak who actually performed the task. Unfortunately, Wozniak's circuit board could not be used as it had no scoring or coin mechanisms.

In December 1978, Bushnell left Atari to create Chuck E. Cheese's Pizza Time Theatre. Kee's Joe Keenan left soon after to help manage the franchise. Former partner Dabney also helped out with this company, which is still a popular food and arcade chain to this day.

The defining transitional point of video game arcade technology was with the release of Midway's Space Invaders game in 1980. This game brought forth with it the power of the microprocessor and the transition from black and white to color graphics. It also brought forth a new wave of a cult phenomenon impact that hadn't been seen since the days of Pong.

The strength of this golden age of video games was solidified with the release of Space Invaders, Asteroids and Pac-Man. This was when color arcade games became more prevalent and individual video arcades devoted to such machines started appearing outside of traditional locales such as bowling alleys or bars. This was the norm through the mid-80s for the video game industry when home video game systems started taking over.

Prior to all of these video games, pinball machines were more popular than video games. The peak year for the pinball industry was 1979 with 200,000 in machine sales and $2.3 billion in revenue. By 1982, this peak declined to 33,000 machines and $464 million in sales.

By this point, Space Invaders and Pac-Man had sold over 360,000 and 400,000 cabinets, respectively, becoming the best-selling machine cabinets for video arcades. Each machine cost around $2000 to $3000 each. Pac-Man's machines were exactly $2400 each.

According to statistics listed in articles such as "Making Millions, 25 cents at a Time" by the Canadian Broadcasting Corporation on November 23, 1982, *Vintage Games* by Bill Loguidice and Matt Barton in 2009 and "Video Game Stars: Pac-Man" by Mark J. P. Wolf in 2008, "Space Invaders grossed $2 billion in quarters by 1982. Pac-Man grossed over $1 billion by 1981 and $2.5 billion by the late 1990s. In 1982, Space Invaders was considered the highest-grossing entertainment product of its time, with comparisons made to the then highest-grossing film *Star Wars*, which had grossed $486 million, while Pac-Man is today considered the highest-grossing arcade game of all time."

Other high-grossing games of this era included Ms. Pac-Man, Asteroids, Donkey Kong, Defender, Galaxian, Donkey Kong Junior, Mr. Do, Tempest, Dragon's Lair, Space Ace, Missile Command, Berserk and others.

The most successful arcade companies at this time were Taito with Space Invaders, Gun Fight and Jungle King; Namco with Pac-Man, Galaxian, Pole Position and Dig Dug; and Atari with Computer Space, Pong and Asteroids. Others included Sega who entered the home console market; Nintendo with Donkey Kong and the various Mario spin-offs and also entered the home console market; and Bally Midway, Cinematronics, Konami, Centuri, Williams and SNK.

Improvements in the arcade games' central processing unit allowed for games to become more complex than earlier games like Pong with discrete circuitry. By the late 1970s, the basic techniques of interactive entertainment were established and their popularity and use drove down hardware prices to such an extent that it helped the PC to become a technology economic reality for both home and work. Also during this time, color monitors and graphics became more widespread following the release of Galaxian in 1979. This experimenting with vector displays produced crisper screen lines that couldn't be duplicated by traditional raster displays, but vector displays fell out of favor due to high repair costs.

Prior to Pac-Man, Space Invaders became the first game after Pong to truly enter popular culture. There was an urban legend that Space Invaders became so popular in Japan, that there was a shortage of 100 Yen coins, but logic disputes this claim that the arcade owners would have taken the Yen coins to the bank and not hold on to them. The reality was that production of new Yen coins was lower during 1978 and 1979 than in other years previous or subsequent.

The impact in Japan soon had a similar impact in North America. After Space Invaders was released, many favorable articles and stories about arcade video games aired on television and were printed in newspapers and magazines. The first video game competition was held in 1980 by Atari and was called The Space Invaders Tournament. The event attracted over 10,000 participants and it established video gaming as a mainstream hobby.

This mainstream hobby influence also had an effect on the music industry. Revenues for the music industry had declined between 1978 and 1981 and this decrease was directly related to the rise of video arcade games at the time. To partially combat this, successful songs based upon video games began appearing. Electronic music band Yellow Magic Orchestra or YMO sampled sounds from the Space Invaders games for their eponymous album and for their hit single called "Computer Game". YMO also had a major influence on video game music produced during the same era.

Space Invaders also inspired "Disco Space Invaders" by Funny Stuff, "Space Invaders" by Playback a.k.a. Player One, "Space Invader" by The Pretenders and "Space Invaders" by Uncle Vic. Playback's song eventually provided the bassline for "On and On" by Jesse Saunders.

Pac-Man's success took everything to the next level. Its release in 1980 caused Pac-Mania, a title that also became the final coin-operated game in the series in 1987. The game was deceptively simple: It featured a yellow, circle-shaped creature who ate dots while going through a maze and trying to avoid his ghost monster enemies. At various intervals, other items appeared such as cherries for Pac-Man to eat. Certain larger dots would make Pac-Man invulnerable for a time so he could eat the ghost monsters for more points. If all the dots were eaten, Pac-Man would then go to the next level and play begins again. As the levels wore on, the ghosts traveled faster and were smarter and the transitioned ghosts lasted for a shorter time.

The popularity of the games spawned numerous clone games, Pac-Man branded foods, toys, an animated television series, and a hit pop song called "Pac-Man Fever" by Buckner and Garcia, which hit #9 on the *Billboard* pop charts Hot 100 and sold over a million copies and a gold record. Buckner and Garcia would have a less successful follow-up with "Do the Donkey Kong". The Pac-Man game was so popular that President Ronald Reagan congratulated a player for setting a record score at the time.

# A Brief History of Arcade Video Games 19

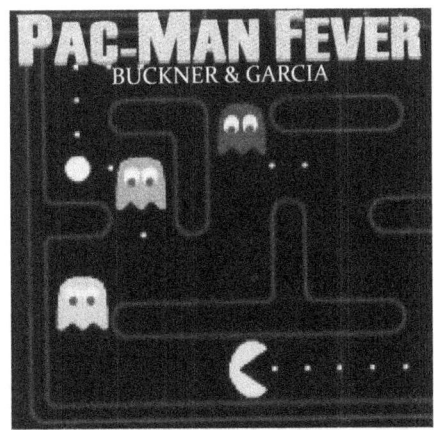

The hit record "Pac-Man Fever" and various other Pac-Man related albums and singles.

Beginning with Space Invaders, video arcade games began appearing at movie theaters, as well as in the movies. Early movies about video games included *Dawn of the Dead* (1978), *Midnight Madness* (1980), *Take This Job and Shove It* (1981), *Puberty Blues* (1981), *TRON* (1982), *Rocky III* (1982), *Fast Times at Ridgemont High* (1982), *Koyaanisqatsi* (1982), *The Toy* (1982), *WarGames* (1983), *Nightmares* (1983), *Joysticks* (1983), *Psycho II* (1983), *Spring Break* (1983), *Never Say Never Again* (1983), *The Last Starfighter* (1984), *Footloose* (1984), *The Karate Kid* (1984), *The Terminator* (1984), *Night of the Comet* (1984), *The Adventures of Buckaroo Banzai* (1984), *Cloak & Dagger* (1984), *The Goonies* (1985), *The Boys Next Door* (1985), *Ferris Bueller's Day Off* (1986), *Something Wild* (1986), *The Color of Money* (1986), *Psycho III* (1986), *Over the Top* (1986), and *Can't Buy Me Love* (1986).

In more recent years, there have been documentaries based on the golden age of video arcade games including *The King of Kong: A Fistful of Quarters* (2007) and *Chasing Ghosts: Beyond the Arcade* (2007) as well as additional feature films capitalizing on the ongoing popularity of video games including *TRON: Legacy* (2010), *Wreck-It Ralph* (2012) and its sequel *Ralph Breaks the Internet* (2018), *Pixels* (2015), *Ready Player One* (2018), *Free Guy* (2021), and retro TV series like *The Goldbergs* and *Stranger Things*.

The popularity of the golden age video games continues to this day.

# A Brief History of Pac-Man

The Japanese video game franchise known as Pac-Man was published, developed and is owned by Bandai Namco Entertainment, formerly known as simply Namco, debuting as an arcade machine in Tokyo's bustling Shibuya district on May 22, 1980. The game entered a field dominated at the time by Midway Games, Atari and Mass Media, Inc. Pac-Man was Namco's first entry into this burgeoning field and was released to video arcades in 1980 by Namco and published by Midway Games for North America.

The game was originally called Puckman due to the popular Japanese phrase for gobbling something up: "Paku paku taberu", with "paku paku" mimicking the sound of a snapping mouth and "taberu" meaning "to eat." When Pac-Man came to America, the name of Puckman was changed to Pac-Man for fear that vandals would scratch the letters on the machines and change the "P" to and "F".

The original Pac-Man was a maze chase game created by Japanese game designer Toru Iwatani. Iwatani said of his invention 40 years later in an article for CNN on May 21, 2020 called "Pac-Man at 40: The Eating Icon That Changed Gaming History," "When I started drafting up this project in the late 1970s, the arcades were filled with violent games all about killing aliens," said Iwatani, who was working for Japanese games firm Namco at the time. "They were gloomy places where only boys went to hang out. What I wanted to do was make arcades into livelier places that women and couples might enjoy visiting, so I thought it best to design a game with women in mind.

"I had started off assuming that themes like fashion and romance might be best suited for a female audience," said Iwatani. "But then I thought -- and this may have been presumptuous of me -- that women also enjoy the act of eating, or 'taberu' in Japanese, and that's how I found myself centered around this keyword and the act of eating as a concept."

The inspiration for the ghosts came from a Japanese manga called "Little Ghost Q-Taro," which Iwatani read as a child and from the American cartoon character of Casper the Friendly Ghost.

"The relationship between Pac-Man and the ghosts is one that's meant to pit them against each other but only in a very superficial sort of way, that stirs up no real hatred," Iwatani said. "It's a relationship influenced by the ideas of the Tom & Jerry cartoons."

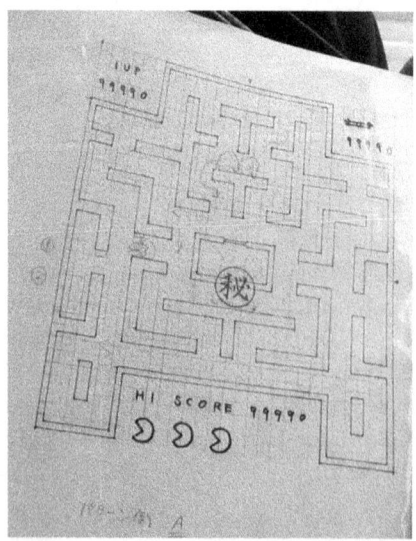

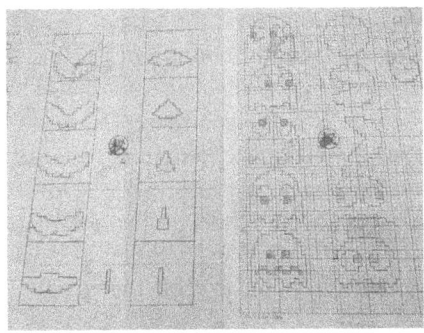 

Photos of Pac-Man designer Toru Iwatani and his original sketches for the first Pac-Man game.

Later on, Pac-Man delved into other video game genres such as platformers, racing and sports. There have been several games made for the series and they have been released both to video arcades and to home consoles and are included in many Namco video game compilations.

Pac-Man has become one of the longest-running, best-selling and highest-grossing video games and video game franchises in history. There have been numerous regular releases over the past 40 years. The games have sold over 48 million copies in all incarnations of the game. This has resulted in a gross of over $14.107 billion in the United States. Most of that total is from the proceeds from the original arcade game.

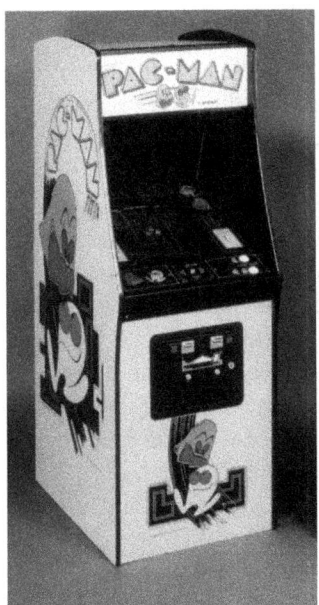 

The original North American arcade versions of Pac-Man and Ms. Pac-Man

Pac-Man as a character has become the official mascot for Bandai Namco and is one of the most recognizable character designs and names in video game history. The Pac-Man franchise is seen as important and influential and the characters are representative of 1980s popular culture and of video games in general.

Ms. Pac-Man debuted in 1982. It is similar to Pac-Man and its first sequel. It was developed by General Computer Corporation and published by Midway and the first not made by Namco. General Computer originally called the game Crazy Otto and it was a modification kit for the original Pac-Man. Because of legal reasons with Atari, General Computer was forced to offer the project to Midway. When Midway purchased it, they told GCC to use the game as a basis for a sequel to Pac-Man. Many names were considered before they settled on Ms. Pac-Man, which was easier to pronounce than Miss Pac-Man or Mrs. Pac-Man. The game was developed without Namco's approval, but Namco's president Masaya Nakamura was consulted about the character design. Namco ultimately ended up collecting the same royalties as they had with Pac-Man. Like Pac-Man, Ms. Pac-Man spawned a great amount of merchandise and was praised for having a female protagonist, as most previous video games had a male one or none. The rights to Ms. Pac-Man are currently owned by Namco's successor company, Bandai Namco Entertainment.

The game play is very similar to Pac-Man except this game has four mazes that appear in different color schemes. Ms. Pac-Man has two warp tunnels instead of one. The game walls are of a solid color rather than an outline making it easier to see the maze paths. The ghosts' movement pattern is more random than predictable. The fruit bonuses also appear randomly and in various places in the maze. Ms. Pac-Man also introduced the ghost named Sue in place of Clyde. Ms. Pac-Man also spins around and dies rather than fold in on himself as Pac-Man does in his game when eaten by a ghost. In the intermissions, Ms. Pac-Man meets the original Pac-Man and eventually we see Baby Pac-Man (who later gets a spin-off game) and the sound effects and music are new. Ultimately, Ms. Pac-Man became even more popular than the original.

Super Pac-Man was going to be the original name of Ms. Pac-Man once it was decided to make Crazy Otto into a Pac-Man game. Over time and many changes, the game became Ms. Pac-Man. Super Pac-Man as a game idea returned in 1982 and was developed and published by Namco and is Namco's official sequel to Pac-Man rather than Ms. Pac-Man which they had little to do with.

The sound, music, special effects and gameplay for Super Pac-Man are dramatically different from the original game. Rather than eat dots, Super Pac-Man eats keys in order to unlock doors. These doors lead to different mazes. There are other items to eat such as more fruit and other prizes such as spaceships. There are also two sizes of power pellets: the standard ones and a larger one that makes Pac-Man super for a short time. While super, Pac-Man becomes much larger and can move with super speed. He is also invulnerable to ghosts. He still can only eat the ghosts in the same standard way of eating the special power pellets designed for eating ghosts. Bonus points can also be scored by eating stars. There are also different bonus levels full of food items and there are no ghosts.

There have been many more variations of Pac-Man created since, but these were the ones that started it all off over 40 years ago and were the basis for the Hanna-Barbera series.

Various magazines, books and toys featuring Pac-Man.

## 26 ▪ The First Animated TV Show Based Upon a Video Game

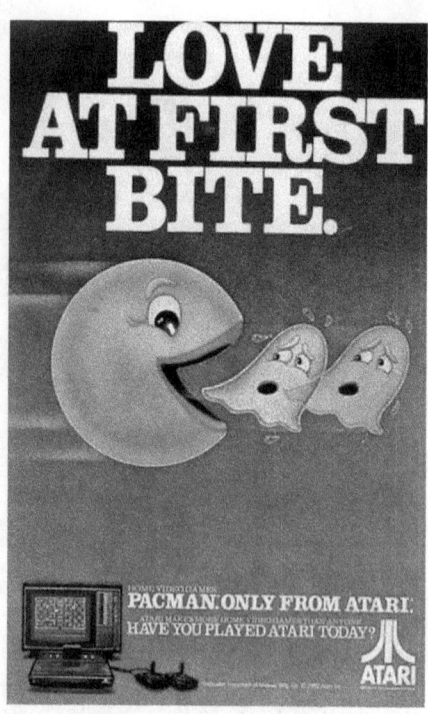

# A Brief History of The Pac-Man Cartoon Show by Hanna-Barbera

The *Pac-Man* cartoon show was a Hanna-Barbera production. It was based on the Namco video games of *Pac-Man*, *Ms. Pac-Man* and *Super Pac-Man*. There were 44 episodes made of the show that aired over two seasons from 1982 through 1984 on ABC TV's Saturday morning schedule. It was the first animated cartoon show based upon a video game.

For the TV series, it followed the adventures of Pac-Man, his wife named Pepper Pac-Man a.k.a. Ms. Pac-Man, with Pac-Baby, their male child, plus their dog named Chomp-Chomp and their cat named Sour Puss. All of the characters live in Pac-Land, a land where everything seems to revolve around circular ball-like shapes. Many of the episodes of the show focus on the ongoing battle between the Pac family and their adversaries, the ghost monsters that go by the name of Inky, Pinky, Blinky, Clyde and Sue. The ghosts work for Mezmaron and their goal is to find and take control of the land's source of Power Pellets. These pellets serve as the main food and power source for the city. The second season of the show also featured the superheroic Super-Pac and Pac-Man's teenage cousin who was named P.J.

One of the fun things about the show is its use of music and sound effects. Music was the same "Turkey in the Straw" cues as used in the actual video games and sound effects were courtesy of the Hanna-Barbara sound library using a lot of existing sounds from the past including many from *The Jetsons* TV series for their car motors and such.

Later Namco games and packaging were based upon or influenced by the Pac-Man cartoon show. Example games included *Pac-Land, Pac-Man 2: The New Adventures* and the Tengen release of the original *Pac-Man* game in a version made for the Nintendo Entertainment System. This release featured box art based upon the Hanna-Barbera series.

Due to the success of the show on ABC, CBS was inspired to create *Saturday Supercade*, produced by Ruby-Spears, which featured other video game characters such as Frogger, Donkey Kong, Donkey Kong Jr., Q*Bert and Pitfall Harry.

Amazingly, even though the series was a success, neither season was solely a Pac-Man show. The first season was called *The Pac-Man/Little Rascals/Richie Rich Show*. It was a 90-minute show that aired on Saturdays from September 25, 1982 - September 3, 1983. The Little Rascals segment was new and based upon the old Hal Roach live-action short series from 1922-1944 originally called *Our Gang*. Richie Rich as a segment had already aired as part of *The Richie Rich/Scooby-Doo Show* from 1980-1982, but these segments were also brand new.

Season one was released on DVD by Warner Archives on January 31, 2012.

For Pac-Man's second season, the show was shortened to 60 minutes and renamed *The Pac-Man/Rubik, the Amazing Cube Hour* which aired on Saturdays from September 10, 1983 - September 1, 1984. The Rubik segment was produced by Ruby-Spears. This second season introduces two new characters: Super-Pac, who is a well-meaning, but somewhat dimwitted superhero who comes to Pac-Land via his time hole in the sky, and P.J., who is a character modeled after TV's Fonz from *Happy Days*, a series that was still amazingly popular at this time.

Season two was released on DVD by Warner Archives on September 11, 2012.

There were also two primetime TV specials produced. The first special was a half-hour show called *The Pac-Man Halloween Special* and consisted of two repeat segments from the series: one called "Pacula" and one called "Trick or Chomp" which originally aired on October 16, 1982. The special originally aired on ABC on October 30, 1982 and replayed over the years on channels such as Cartoon Network or Boomerang during Halloween time in subsequent years.

The second primetime special was an all-new half-hour special called *Christmas Comes to Pac-Land*. It originally aired on ABC on December 16, 1982. It tells the story of how Pac-Man and his family help Santa Claus after he crash lands in Pac-Land. The special was released on VHS and is now available for streaming through Amazon Prime, and is part of the season two DVD. It still airs every December on Boomerang.

Since its original run, the series has run in syndication as well as on USA Cartoon Express in the 1980s, Cartoon Network from 1995-1999, and Boomerang from 2000-2014.

*Pac-Man and his Ghostly Adventures* was a sequel animated TV series. 52 episodes were produced over three seasons from June 15, 2013 – May 29, 2015. It originally aired on Disney XD and later was released to home video. The series is also known as *Pac-World* and it was produced by 41 Entertainment, Arad Productions and Bandai Namco Entertainment.

This series took place on and around the planet called Pac-World and also Nether-World. The same characters from earlier versions of Pac-Man appear including Blinky, Pinky, Inky, Clyde and Count Pacula, plus a number of new ones including Cylindria, Spiraltron, Betrayus, President Stratos Spheros, Sir Cumference, Skeebo, Spheria Suprema, Ms. Globular, Mr. Strictler, Mr. Dome, O'Drool, Kingpin Obtuse, Rotunda, Zac, Sunny, The Pacinator, Do-Ug, Danny Vaincori, Elliptika, Moondog, Starchild, Grannie, Santa Pac, Butt-ler, Dr. A.H. Buttocks, Glooky, Mavis, Specter, Fred, Master Goo, Captain Banshee, Cyclops, Ghosteroid, other various ghosts, Apex, Professor Pointy Brains, Tip, Grinder, Grindette, Grinder-Tron, Mega-Grinder, Computer Bug, Pac-Topus, Cyber-Mouse, Cyber-Fluffy, Madame Ghoulasha, Jean, Mooby, The Easter Pac-Peep, Mummy Wizard, Round Deer, Dr. Pacenstein Fluffy, Fuzbitz, Hugefoot and various other monsters. The series had a 3-D animated look rather than the flat cel-animation used for Hanna-Barbera's animated Pac-Man series. Pepper, Pac-Baby, Chomp-Chomp, Sour Puss, Dinky, Sue and Mezmaron do not appear from the earlier series.

## A Brief History of The Pac-Man Cartoon Show by Hanna-Barbera

An ad promoting Pac-Man on Saturday mornings.

**34** ■ *The First Animated TV Show Based Upon a Video Game*

Typical title card for Pac-Man episode.

Ads and images for Pac-Man holiday specials.

**36** ■ *The First Animated TV Show Based Upon a Video Game*

The Pac-Man DVDs from Warner Archives.

# A Brief History of The Pac-Man Cartoon Show by Hanna-Barbera

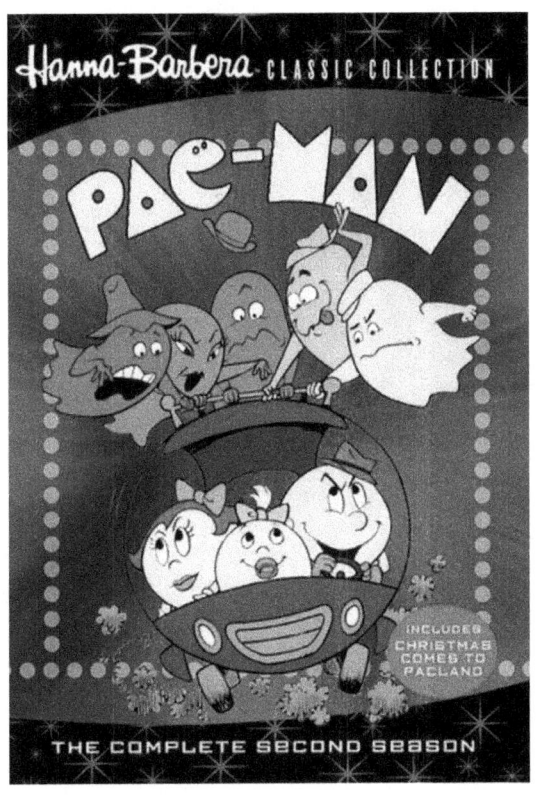

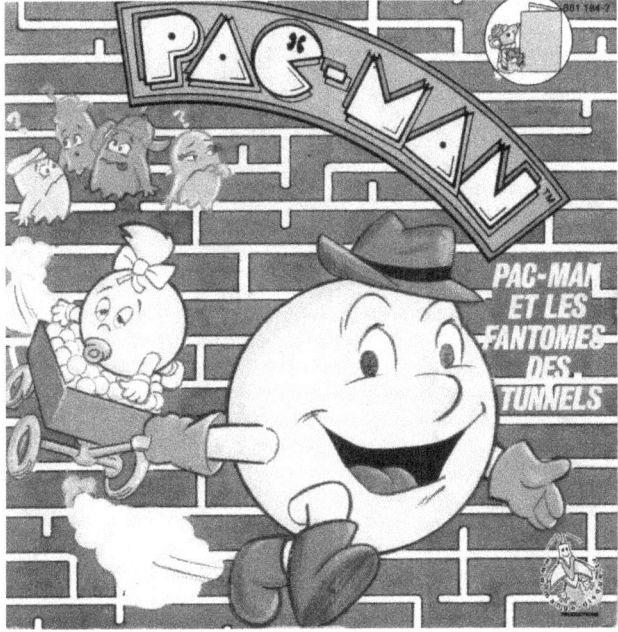

Pac-Man book tie-ins.

## The First Animated TV Show Based Upon a Video Game

Pac-Man Valentines.

# Who's Who on The Pac-Man Cartoon Show

## VOICE CAST:

Marty Ingels

## The First Animated TV Show Based Upon a Video Game

Pac-Man

# Marty Ingels (March 9, 1936 - October 21, 2015): Pac-Man

Ingels was an actor, comedian, comedy sketch writer, theatrical agent and voice artist. He was best known as the co-star of the TV series *I'm Dickens, He's Fenster*. He also appeared on TV's *The Phil Silvers Show*, *The Ann Sothern Show*, *Pete and Gladys*, *Manhunt*, *Hennesey*, *The Dick Van Dyke Show*, *The Joey Bishop Show*, *Burke's Law*, *The Addams Family*, *Bewitched*, *The Phyllis Diller Show*, *Good Morning World*, *The Partners*, *Banacek*, *The Rookies*, *Adam-12*, *The Ghost Busters*, *Police Story*, *Chips*, *The Love Boat*, *Family*, *The Munsters Today*, *The New Adam-12*, *Murder She Wrote*, *Baywatch*, *Walker Texas Ranger*, *ER*, *CSI*, and the movies *The Ladies Man*, *The Busy Body*, *A Guide for the Married Man*, *If It's Tuesday, It Must Be Belgium*, and *Linda Lovelace for President*. For Hanna-Barbera, Ingels also did the voice of Autocat for *Motormouse and Autocat* as part of *The Cattanooga Cats*, and Beegle Beagle for *The Great Grape Ape Show* a.k.a. *The Tom & Jerry/Grape Ape Show*, plus the Devil for Disney's *Darkwing Duck*. He was married to actress Shirley Jones from 1977-2015.

Shirley explains got the role of Pac-Man in *Shirley & Marty: An Unlikely Love Story*, "Marty even stumbled into a second career in 1980. He came back to the public ear, if not the public eye, as the voice of Pac-Man, a cartoon favorite of millions of American grade-schoolers.

"Of course, he thought he was through with that end of show business. His return was the kind of fateful accident that seemed to characterize so much of his world. He was sitting at his desk one morning, hustling one of his clients, Robert Culp, who had starred with Bill Cosby in the *I Spy* series. He heard Universal was casting a film, and he dialed what he thought was the studio's number. He was a digit or two off, and instead he reached Hanna-Barbera, the producers of animated cartoons and other Disney-like features.

"Instead of hanging up, Marty figured why waste a phone call? He asked who their casting director was, and the operator put him through to a man named Gordon Hunt. No sooner had he introduced himself than a baffled Ingels heard Hunt tell him, excitedly, 'You know, after two years of trying, we finally landed the rights to Pac-Man.'

"Here's Marty with the rest of the story:

"And I said, 'Wow!' I had not the foggiest idea what Pac-Man was. For all I knew, it was a luggage company. So I said, 'Well, that's wonderful,' and he goes on: 'We have all the other characters, Pac-Baby and Ms. Pac-Man and the ghost monsters, and the only person we don't have is Pac-Man himself. It's very difficult. We've listened to 173 voices, and it has to run through all these approvals.'

"He mentioned this whole bureaucratic system: ABC, and the top brass at Hanna-Barbera, and Bally Midway, the company that owned the patent, and a little Oriental man in Hong Kong who invented the machine.

"So I said to him, 'Robert Culp would be sensational for you,' And Hunt said to me, 'Would you say that again?'

"I said, 'Say what again?'

"'What you just said, the thing about Culp.'

"I repeated myself, 'Robert Culp would be perfect for the part,' I felt as confident as one can feel, without knowing anything at all about the part itself.

"Hunt asked me what I was doing at that moment. I told him I was sitting in my office. He got as far as, 'Could you come down to…' and I cut him short. I said, 'I don't come anywhere. I don't go anywhere.'

"He said, 'Well, I would like to put your voice down on tape, because I think you have a great voice.'

"I said, 'You don't understand. I don't compete anymore. I don't get disappointed anymore. I don't get hurt anymore. I don't have to shave anymore. I hang around in my pajamas all day. I don't have to be Tom Selleck or Robin Williams or anybody.'

"It turned out he was taping my voice while we were talking. Two days later, my secretary said, 'A Mr. Gordon Hunt, the guy who may have a job for Robert Culp.'

"I picked up the phone and said, 'You find anything for Culp?' He said, 'No, but I have a job for you, starting tomorrow at ten o'clock in the morning.'

"During the nearly two years it lasted, Pac-Man turned out to be a dream job. I could drive to the studio in my pajamas and do three weeks' worth of voice-overs in one afternoon. I made more money as a cartoon than I did in my entire career as a comedian."

Shirley Jones added in her book *Shirley Jones: A Memoir*, "Marty does, indeed, have a remarkable voice, strong, rich, gravelly, and with a marked Brooklyn accent."

Pepper

## Barbara Minkus (February 20, 1942 - ): Pepper Pac-Man

Minkus was best-known for her appearances on *Love, American Style*, on which she appeared 27 times, mainly as a bit player on the in-between segments that were only on the first season. Of the 27, two were parts in actual segments. She was also the original Lucy in the stage production of *You're a Good Man, Charlie Brown*. Other TV shows she appeared on included *The Governor and J.J.*, *That Girl*, *Curiosity Shop*, *Lotsa Luck!*, *Rhoda*, *Baretta*, *Alice*, *Family Ties*, *You Again?*, and the movies *Lady Sings the Blues*, *Bob & Carol & Ted & Alice*, *Linda Lovelace for President*, *The Happy Hooker Goes to Washington*, and *Mother, Juggs & Speed*.

## Russi Taylor (May 4, 1944 - July 26, 2019): Pac-Baby

Taylor was best known for voicing Minnie Mouse for 33 years from 1986-2019, and for various voices on *The Simpsons* including Martin Prince, purple-haired twins Sherri and Terri, and German exchange student Üter. She was married to Wayne Allwine from 1991-2009, who was the voice of Mickey Mouse for 32 years. She also voiced Webigail Vanderquack and Huey, Dewey and Louie on the original *DuckTales* TV series. Other voices included Pebbles Flintstone on *The Flintstone Comedy Hour*, Strawberry Shortcake, Baby Gonzo on *Muppet Babies*, Birdie the Early Bird for McDonald's commercials, and dozens of other voices.

Pac-Baby

Mezmaron

## Allan Lurie (July 25, 1923 - March 10, 2015): Mezmaron

Lurie voiced for a number of other Hanna-Barbera productions, usually listed as additional voices. Shows include *A Pup Named Scooby-Doo, Foofer, Midnight Patrol: Adventures in the Dream Zone, Pink Panther and Sons, Popeye and Son, Richie Rich, Space Stars, The Adventures of Don Coyote and Sancho Panda, The Flintstone Kids, The Jetsons, The New Yogi Bear Show, The Smurfs*, and *Tom & Jerry Kids*. As an onscreen actor, he appeared in *General Electric Theater, The Texan, Gunsmoke, The Danny Thomas Show, The Twilight Zone, The Girl from U.N.C.L.E., The Bold Ones, All in the Family, Grady, Emergency!, Sanford, Voyagers!, Insight, St. Elsewhere, Hill Street Blues*, and *The Hughleys*.

## Neil Ross (December 31, 1944 - ): Clyde

Ross was a British-born, Canadian-American voice actor and announcer. He has announced for numerous *Playboy Video Playmate Calendar* videos, *Biography, The Academy Awards, The Emmy Awards, The Golden Globe Awards*, and *Nova*. His cartoon voice work includes *Spider-Man, Pandamonium, Mork & Mindy/Laverne & Shirley/Fonz Hour, Richie Rich, The Dukes, Rubik the Amazing Cube, The New Scooby-Doo and Scrappy-Doo Show, Spider-Man and his Amazing Friends, G.I. Joe, Pole Position, The Jetsons, Voltron, Punky Brewster, Paw Paws, Kissyfur, Jem, The Transformers, Wildfire, Hulk Hogan's Rock 'n' Wrestling, An*

Clyde                                    Sue

*American Tail, Galaxy High School, Centurions, Inhumanoids, Rambo, Sectaurs, The Brave Little Toaster, The Smurfs, Mighty Mouse: The New Adventures, The Transformers, Bionic Six, The Real Ghostbusters, Visionaries, DuckTales, CBS Storybreak, Superman, Little Nemo, The Karate Kid, Fantastic Max, Little Dracula, Attack of the Killer Tomatoes, Yo Yogi!, ProStars, Fish Police, Capitol Critters, Ferngully, ABC Weekend Specials, Darkwing Duck, Mr. Bogus, Tom & Jerry Kids, Mother Goose and Grimm, Prince Valiant, The Pirates of Dark Water, The Little Mermaid, Bonkers, Batman, Cowboys of Moo Mesa, Thumbelina, Animaniacs, Rugrats, Mighty Max, Garfield and Glo Friends, Aladdin, SWAT Kats, Biker Mice from Mars, Daisy-Head Mayzie, The Pebble and the Penguin, Freakazoid!, Dumb and Dumber, Sylvester & Tweety Mysteries, Iron Man, Fantastic Four, Hyperman, Twisted Tales of Felix the Cat, Quack Pack, Mortal Kombat, Savage Dragon, The Mask, The Blues Brothers, New Batman Adventures, Pinky and the Brain, Zorro, Star Wars, Da Mob, My Life as a Teenage Robot, Harvey Birdman Attorney at Law, Ben 10,* and *Kung Fu Panda.*

## Susan Silo (July 27, 1942 - ): Sue

Silo started her career as an onscreen actress appearing on *The Jack Benny Program, The Many Loves of Dobie Gillis, The Ann Sothern Show, Sea Hunt, Alfred Hitchcock Presents, The New Breed, Route 66, Hawaiian Eye, Hazel, Wagon Train, Have Gun Will Travel, The Lieutenant, Harry's Girls, McHale's Navy, Burke's Law, Combat!, Bonanza, Valentine's Day, The Wild Wild West, The Man from U.N.C.L.E., Batman, Dr. Kildare, My Three Sons, Gunsmoke, Here Come the Brides, The Love Boat, Highway to Heaven,* and *LA Law.* For voicework, she appeared on *Yes Virginia, There is a Santa Claus, CB Bears, The Fonz and the Happy Days Gang, Kidd Video, The Glo Friends, Inhumanoids, Foofer, The Smurfs, Fantastic Max, Captain Planet and the Planeteers, The Adventures of Don Coyote and Sancho Panda, Jetsons: The Movie, TaleSpin, Toxic Crusaders, Attack of the Killer Tomatoes, Where's Waldo?, Prince Valiant, Spacecats, ProStars, James Bond Jr., Darkwing Duck, Tom & Jerry Kids, Super Dave, All-New Dennis the Menace, The Pink Panther, Garfield and Glo Friends, Daisy-Head Mayzie, Biker Mice from Mars, The Tick, Twisted Tales of Felix the Cat, Richie Rich, SpyDogs, Jakers! The Adventures of Piggley Winks, Avatar: The Last Airbender, Xiaolin Showdown, Curious George, The Legend of Korra, Blaze and the Monster Machines,* and *The Tom & Jerry Show.*

Inky

## Barry Gordon (December 21, 1948 - ): Inky

Gordon was an actor, political talk show host and the longest-serving President of the Screen Actors Guild, serving from 1988-1995. In films, he appeared in *The Girl Can't Help It*, *Cinderfella*, *Hands of a Stranger*, *A Thousand Clowns*, *The Spirit is Willing*, and *Love at First Bite*. TV shows include *The Jack Benny Program*, *The Danny Thomas Show*, *The Ann Sothern Show*, *Leave it to Beaver*, *Alfred Hitchcock Presents*, *Dennis the Menace*, *Thriller*, *Dr. Kildare*, *The Smothers Brothers Show*, *Love American Style*, *The Don Rickles Show*, *The New Dick Van Dyke Show*, *Mannix*, *Kolchak*, *The Bob Crane Show*, *The Practice*, *Fish*, *The Incredible Hulk*, *Supertrain*, *Barney Miller*, *Three's Company*, *I'm a Big Girl Now*, *Archie Bunker's Place*, *Star Trek: Deep Space Nine*, *LA Law*, *NYPD Blue*, *Empty Nest*, *Caroline in the City*, *The Hughleys*, *Star Trek: Voyager*, *Becker*, *Dragnet*, and *Curb Your Enthusiasm*. Voice acting includes *Jabberjaw*, *Tarzan*, *The Kid Super Power Hour with Shazam!*, *Meatballs & Spaghetti*, *Snorks*, *The Jetsons*, *The Smurfs*, *Teenage Mutant Ninja Turtles*, *Superman*, *Gravedale High*, *Darkwing Duck*, *Space Cats*, *A Pup Named Scooby-Doo*, *Tom & Jerry Kids*, *Droopy Master Detective*, *Batman*, *SWAT Kats*, and *The Pink Panther*.

Blinky            Pinky

# Chuck McCann (September 2, 1934 - April 8, 2018): Blinky, Pinky

McCann was an actor, voice artist, comedian, puppeteer, commercial presenter and TV host. In movies, he appeared in *The Heart is a Lonely Hunter, Herbie Rides Again, Linda Lovelace for President, Silent Movie, They Went That-a-Way and That-a-Way, Hamburger: The Motion Picture, Ladybugs, Robin Hood: Men in Tights, Dracula: Dead and Loving In*, and *I Know That Voice*. On TV, he appeared on *The Chuck McCann Show, Columbo, Little House on the Prairie, Far Out Space Nuts, All That Glitters, Starsky and Hutch, The Rockford Files, The Greatest American Hero, Santa Barbara*, and *Invasion*. For voice acting, he appeared on *Cool McCool, CB Bears, Fred and Barney Meet the Shmoo, Scooby-Doo and Scrappy-Doo, The Plastic Man Comedy/Adventure Show, Captain Caveman and the Teen Angels, Drak Pack, Super Friends, Thundarr the Barbarian, Space Stars, Richie Rich, The Get Along Gang, Snorks, The Jetsons, Galtar and the Golden Lance, G.I. Joe, Pound Puppies, A Pup Named Scooby-Doo, The Smurfs, Fantastic Max, Chip 'n' Dale's Rescue Rangers, Adventures of the Gummi Bears, DuckTales, The New Adventures of Winnie the Pooh, TaleSpin, Garfield and Friends, Attack of the Killer Tomatoes, Toxic Crusaders, Tom & Jerry Kids, Animaniacs, All-New Dennis the Menace, Droopy Master Detective, ABC Weekend Special, Fantastic Four, Twisted Tales of Felix the Cat, What a Cartoon!, Iron Man, Duckman, The Tick, The Incredible Hulk, The Powerpuff Girls*, and *Adventure Time*. Plus, he appeared in Right Guard commercials where he said the catchphrase, "Hi, Guy!"

Sour Puss

## Peter Cullen (July 28, 1941 - ): Sour Puss

Cullen is Canadian voice actor best known as the voice of Optimus Prime from *The Transformers* and Eeyore in the later *Winnie the Pooh* films. His vocal performances in feature films include *King Kong, Heidi's Song, Gremlins, Rainbow Brite and the Star Stealer, Voltron, Heathcliff, GoBots, My Little Pony, G.I. Joe, Rockin' with Judy Jetson, Yogi and the Invasion of the Space Bears, Pooh's Grand Adventure, The Tigger Movie, Piglet's Big Movie, Pooh's Heffalump Movie*, and *Bumblebee*. For TV, he did voices for *The Jetsons, The Smothers Brothers Comedy Hour, Mighty Man and Yukk, Scooby-Doo and Scrappy-Doo, The Kwicky Koala Show, The Smurfs, Spider-Man and his Amazing Friends, The Scooby & Scrappy-Doo/Puppy Hour, Spider-Man, Meatballs & Spaghetti, The Little Rascals, Monchichis, The Puppy's Further Adventures, The Biskitts, Saturday Supercade, The Dukes, Mister T, Dungeons & Dragons, Dragon's Lair, Heathcliff, Snorks, Rainbow Brite, Alvin and the Chipmunks, Lucky Luke, The Transformers, Voltron, Challenge of the GoBots, G.I. Joe, Rambo, Muppet Babies, Ghostbusters, Pound Puppies, The New Adventures of Jonny Quest, Foofer, My Little Pony, Bravestarr, DuckTales, The Real Ghostbusters, Dino-Riders, The New Yogi Bear Show, The New Adventures of Winnie the Pooh, Adventures of the Gummi Bears, Teenage Mutant Ninja Turtles, Rude Dog and the Dweebs, Chip 'n' Dale's Rescue Rangers, TaleSpin, Tom & Jerry Kids, The Pirates of Dark Water, Bonkers, House of Mouse, The Book of Winnie the Pooh*. Live-action TV appearances include *The Sonny and Cher Comedy Hour, The Hudson Brothers Razzle Dazzle Show, The Sonny Comedy Revue, The Wolfman Jack Show, Three's a Crowd*, and *In Living Color*.

Chomp-Chomp

# Frank Welker (March 12, 1946 - ): Chomp-Chomp, Morris, Adult Pac-Baby

Welker was primarily a voice artist, but also a live-action actor and a stand-up comedian. His onscreen appearances include *The Trouble with Girls, The Computer Wore Tennis Shoes, How to Frame a Figg, Now You See Him Now You Don't,* and *The Informant.* Live-action TV includes *The Partridge Family, The Paul Lynde Show, Butch Cassidy, Wonderbug,* and *The Banana Splits.* For TV commercials, Welker has been Dig'em Frog for Honey Smacks, Grimace for McDonald's, and Crackle for Rice Krispies. For TV cartoons, he has done voices for *Scooby-Doo, Where Are You?, The New Scooby-Doo Movies, The ABC Saturday Superstar Movie, Bailey's Comets, Super Friends, Valley of the Dinosaurs, Partridge Family 2200 A.D., Hong Kong Phooey, Wheelie and the Chopper Bunch, The Scooby-Doo/Dynomutt Hour, Jabberjaw, ABC Weekend Special, The Robonic Stooges, Laff-a-Lympics, Captain Caveman and the Teen Angels, Dinky Dog, Fangface, Yogi's Space Race, The New Fantastic Four, The New Adventures of Mighty Mouse and Heckle & Jeckle, Buford and the Galloping Ghost, The New Shmoo, The Super Globetrotters, The Flintstones Comedy Show, The Richie Rich/Scooby-Doo Show, The Tom & Jerry Comedy Show, Sport Billy, Fonz and the Happy Days Gang, Space Stars, Trollkins, Blackstar, The Kwicky Koala Show, The Smurfs, Spider-Man and his Amazing Friends, Mork & Mindy/Laverne & Shirley/Fonz Hour, Richie Rich, The Littles, Inspector Gadget, Dungeons & Dragons, Saturday Supercade, The Get Along Gang, Muppet Babies, Snorks, The Transformers, Challenge of the GoBots, The Jetsons, Paw Paws, G.I. Joe, Rambo, Kissyfur, Foofer, The Flintstone Kids, Pound Puppies, The Real Ghostbusters, Bionic Six, DuckTales, Garfield and Friends, Superman, The Completely Mental Misadventures of Ed Grimley, This is America Charlie Brown, Chip 'n' Dale's Rescue Rangers, The Further Adventures of SuperTed, Dink the Little Dinosaur, TaleSpin, Bobby's World, Tom & Jerry Kids, Tiny Toon Adventures, The Adventures of Don Coyote and Sancho Panda, Captain Planet and the Planeteers, The Pirates of Dark Water, The Simpsons, Darkwing Duck, Where's Waldo?, Capitol Critters, Fish Police, Goof Troop, Batman, The Little Mermaid, Bonkers, SWAT Kats, Animaniacs, Droopy Master Detective, Marsupilami, Sonic the Hedgehog, Aladdin, Gargoyles, The Magic School Bus, The Shnookums and Meat Funny Cartoon Show, Dumb and Dumber, The Mask, Timon and Pumbaa, Sylvester and Tweety Mysteries, Freakazoid!, Pinky and the Brain, Dexter's Laboratory, The Spooktacular New Adventures of Casper, The Real Adventures of Jonny Quest, Quack Pack, The Mighty Ducks, Gargoyles, Road Rovers, Cave Kids, Jungle Cubs, Waynehead, Superman, Johnny Bravo, 101 Dalmatians, Hercules, Histeria!, The Powerpuff Girls, The Wild Thornberrys, I Am Weasel, Family Guy, Futurama, Cow and Chicken, Recess, Batman Beyond, Buzz Lightyear, CatDog, House of Mouse, SpongeBob SquarePants, The Grim Adventures of Billy & Mandy, Harvey Birdman Attorney at Law, Kim Possible, Lilo & Stitch, Duck Dodgers, Danny Phantom, The Emperor's New School, Curious George, Robot Chicken, The*

*Garfield Show, Pound Puppies, Mad, The Tom & Jerry Show, Guardians of the Galaxy,* and *Press Your Luck,* plus dozens and dozens of characters, sounds and narration for the movies.

## Lennie Weinrib (April 29, 1935 - June 28, 2006): Pacula

Weinrib was an actor, voice actor, comedian and writer. He was best known for voicing H.R. Pufnstuf, Grimace for McDonald's commercials, Cookie Jarvis for Cookie Crisp cereal, Inch High Private Eye, Scrappy-Doo, Bigmouth, and Timer for *Time for Timer*. TV shows he appeared on include *The Dick Van Dyke Show, My Favorite Martian, The Man from U.N.C.L.E., Happy Days, The Krofft Supershow, Laredo, Adam-12, Emergency!, The Munsters, The Waltons, The Twilight Zone,* and *Alfred Hitchcock Presents*. He also appeared in the films of *Tales of Terror, The Thrill of it All, It's a Mad Mad Mad Mad World, Not with My Wife, You Don't, Good Times, Out of Sight, Bedknobs and Broomsticks,* and *The Strongest Man in the World*. He also did voices for *Lidsville, The Skatebirds, Barnyard Commandos, Buford and the Galloping Ghost, CB Bears, Dr. Dolittle, Dynomutt, Foofer, Galaxy Goof-Ups, Garfield and Friends, Help It's the Hair Bear Bunch, Hong Kong Phooey, Jabberjaw, Jokebook, Kissyfur, Mork & Mindy/Laverne & Shirley/Fonz Hour, My Little Pony, Rambo, Space Cats, Space Stars, The Addams Family, Adventures of the Gummi Bears, The Adventures of Don Coyote and Sancho Panda, The Brady Kids, The All-New Popeye Hour, The Amazing Chan and the Chan Clan, The Most Important Person, The Flintstone Kids, The Further Adventures of SuperTed, The Great Grape Ape Show, The Hoober-Bloob Highway, The Jetsons, The Kwicky Koala Show, The Little Rascals, Batman, The Pebbles and Bamm-Bamm Show, The Pink Panther Laugh-and-a-Half, Hour and a Half Show, The Plastic Man Comedy/Adventure Show, The Smurfs, The Super Globetrotters, The Tom & Jerry Show, These Are the Days, Trollkins, Uncle Croc's Block, Voltron, Wheelie and the Chopper Bunch, Yogi's Gang, Yogi's Space Race,* and *Yogi's Treasure Hunt*.

### SEASON TWO VOICES:

## Darryl Hickman (July 28, 1931 - ): P.J.

Hickman started as a child actor and was the older brother of Dwayne Hickman. He was also a voice artist, screenwriter, TV executive and acting coach. As an actor, he appeared in *The Prisoner of Zenda, The Grapes of Wrath, The Farmer's Daughter, Men of Boys Town, Northwest Ranger, The Human Comedy, Meet Me in St. Louis, Boys' Ranch, A Kiss for Corliss, Destination Gobi, Southwest Passage, The*

P.J.

*Iron Sheriff, The Tingler, Network,* and *Sharky's Machine.* On TV, he appeared on *The Life and Legend of Wyatt Earp, Perry Mason, Climax!, Alfred Hitchcock Presents, Tales of Wells Fargo, Gunsmoke, The Millionaire, The Many Loves of Dobie Gillis, The Loretta Young Show, Rawhide, The Untouchables, Dr. Kildare, Love American Style, Maude, All in the Family, Beauty and the Beast, Baywatch,* and *The Nanny.* He did voices for *Space Stars, The Biskitts, Challenge of the GoBots, Pole Position, The Greatest Adventure: Stories from the Bible, Wildfire, The New Adventures of Jonny Quest,* and *A Pup Named Scooby-Doo.*

Pepper, Sue, Dinky

## Julie McWhirter (October 12, 1947 - ): Dinky

McWhirter was a voice actress and actress. She married DJ and host Rick Dees in 1977. Her onscreen TV appearances include *Happy Days, The Bobby Darin Show, The Hollywood Squares, The Rich Little Show, The Mike Douglas Show, The Dean Martin Celebrity Roast, The Alan Hamel Show, Wacko, The Alan Thicke Show, The John Davidson Show,* and *TV Bloopers & Practical Jokes.* Her voice work includes *The Barkleys, Jeannie, The New Scooby-Doo Movies, Partridge Family 2200 A.D., Clue Club, The Scooby-Doo/Dynomutt Hour, Jabberjaw, Captain Caveman and the Teen Angels, CB Bears, The Skatebirds, Fred Flintstone and Friends, Casper and the Angels, The Plastic Man Comedy/Adventure Show, Drak Pack, Thundarr the Barbarian, Laverne & Shirley in the Army, Pandamonium, The Gary Coleman Show, Mork & Mindy/Laverne & Shirley/Fonz Hour, The Little Rascals, Super Friends, ABC Weekend Specials, Alvin and the Chipmunks, Saturday Supercade, The Smurfs, The Littles, The Jetsons, The Flintstone Kids, The Pirates of Dark Water,* and *Bobby's World.*

Super-Pac

## Lorenzo Music (May 2, 1937 - August 4, 2001): Super-Pac

Music was the original voice of Garfield and was the voice of Carlton the Doorman on *Rhoda* and for the *Carlton Your Doorman* animated pilot. He also was co-creator of *The Bob Newhart Show*. As an actor, he appeared on *The Smothers Brothers Comedy Hour*. As a writer, he wrote for *The Leslie Uggams Show, Love American Style, The Mary Tyler Moore Show, The Bob Newhart Show, Rhoda,* and *Rugrats*. He also provided voices for *The GLO Friends, Fluppy Dogs, The Real Ghostbusters, The Jetsons, Pound Puppies, Fantastic Max, TaleSpin, Darkwing Duck, Rugrats,* and *The Drew Carey Show*.

## ADDITIONAL VOICES:

### William Callaway (March 11, 1940 - )

Callaway was a voice actor best known for playing Aquaman on *Super Friends*. In live-action, he appeared on *That Girl, The Wild Wild West, Gomer Pyle, Gunsmoke, Love American Style, Fun with Dick and Jane, Annie Hall, Rabbit Test, Taxi, Chips, Eight is Enough,* and *The Incredible Hulk*. For voice over,

cast

he appeared on *Cattanooga Cats, Help It's the Hair Bear Bunch, Sealab 2020, Scooby-Doo and Scrappy-Doo, Captain Caveman and the Teen Angels, Drak Pack, The Richie Rich/Scooby-Doo Show, Trollkins, The Smurfs, The Little Rascals, Spider-Man and his Amazing Friends, Mork & Mindy/Laverne & Shirley/Fonz Hour, The Dukes, Challenge of the GoBots, Lucky Luke, Galtar and the Golden Lance, My Little Pony, G.I. Joe, Defenders of the Earth, Inhumanoids, Yogi's Great Escape, Foofer, DuckTales, Jem, The New Yogi Bear Show, Superman, Fantastic Max, Camp Candy, Darkwing Duck, ProStars, Tom & Jerry Kids, Bonkers, Droopy: Master Detective,* and *Quack Pack.*

## Jodi Carlisle (August 28, 1960 - )

Carlisle was a voice actress best known as one of the principal voice actors on *The Wild Thornberrys*. She appeared in live-action on *Night Court, Mad About You, Arliss, 7th Heaven, Judging Amy, Malcolm in the Middle, The Bold and the Beautiful, CSI: Miami, That 70s Show, Big Love, Medium, Cold Case, Ugly Betty, Desperate Housewives, Criminal Minds,* and *Superstore*. Other voice work includes *The New Scooby-Doo Mysteries, ABC Weekend Specials, Hulk Hogan's Rock 'n' Wrestling, The Real Ghostbusters, Dink the Little Dinosaur, TaleSpin, Darkwing Duck, Prince Valiant, Goof Troop, Bonkers, Cowboys of Moo Mesa, Duckman, Rugrats, Avatar: The Last Airbender, Robot Chicken,* and *The Mr. Peabody & Sherman Show.*

## Brian Cummings (March 4, 1948 - )

Cummings was a voice actor and announcer for various radio and TV commercials and TV and motion picture promos. Cartoons shows he has worked on include *Spider-Man, The Little Rascals, The New Scooby and Scrappy-Doo Show, Snorks, Pole Position, The Wuzzles, The Jetsons, The Berenstain Bears, G.I. Joe, Pound Puppies, DuckTales, Adventures of the Gummi Bears, Tom & Jerry Kids, Garfield and Friends, ProStars, 2 Stupid Dogs, Teenage Mutant Ninja Turtles, Animaniacs, The Grim Adventures of Billy & Mandy,* and *The Emperor's New School.*

## Pat Fraley (February 18, 1949 - )

Fraley was a voice actor and a voice-over teacher. Cartoons he did voices for include *Adventures of the Gummi Bears, Aladdin, Alvin and the Chipmunks, Barnyard Commandos, Batman, Biker Mice from Mars, Bill & Ted's Excellent Adventures, Bobby's World, Bonkers, Bravestarr, Camp Candy, The Spooktacular*

*New Adventures of Casper, Cow and Chicken, Darkwing Duck, Droopy: Master Detective, DuckTales, Fantastic Max, Ghostbusters, G.I. Joe, Galaxy High, Galtar and the Golden Lance, Garfield and Friends, Gargoyles, Goof Troop, James Bond Jr., King of the Hill, Kissyfur, Lucky Luke, Men in Black, Muppet Babies, My Little Pony, Paw Paws, Pound Puppies, ProStars, Quack Pack, Rainbow Brite, Raw Toonage, Richie Rich, Saturday Supercade, Scooby-Doo and Scrappy-Doo, Snorks, Sonic the Hedgehog, Space Cats, Spider-Man and his Amazing Friends, Super Friends, TaleSpin, Teenage Mutant Ninja Turtles, The Addams Family, Angry Beavers, The Dukes, The Fairly OddParents, The Flintstone Kids, The Further Adventures of SuperTed, The Glo Friends, The Grim Adventures of Billy & Mandy, The Incredible Hulk, The Jetsons, The Little Mermaid, The Littles, The New Yogi Bear Show, The Secret Files of the Spy Dogs, The Smurfs, The Mask, The Tick, The Twisted Tales of Felix the Cat, Tom & Jerry Kids, Woody Woodpecker, Timon and Pumbaa, Tiny Toon Adventures, Where's Waldo?,* and *Yo Yogi!*

## Joan Gerber (July 29, 1935 - August 22, 2011)

Gerber was a voice actress who is best known as the voice of Freddie the Flute on *H.R. Pufnstuf.* She also voiced for *Matty's Funday Funnies, The Bugs Bunny Show, Roger Ramjet, The Super 6, The Pink Panther Show, Lancelot Link, The Bugaloos, Lidsville, Help It's the Hair Bear Bunch, Wait Till Your Father Gets Home, The Barkleys, The New Scooby-Doo Movies, The Houndcats, Charlotte's Web, These Are the Days, Partridge Family 2200 A.D., The Oddball Couple, The Scooby-Doo/Dynomutt Hour, Clue Club, I Am the Greatest: The Adventures of Muhammad Ali, CB Bears, The New Fantastic Four, The All-New Popeye Hour, The Richie Rich/Scooby-Doo Hour, The Kwicky Koala Show, Heidi's Song, Monchichis, Snorks, DuckTales, Tiny Toon Adventures, Teenage Mutant Ninja Turtles, Gravedale High, Capitol Critters, Goof Troop,* and *Duck Dodgers.*

## Arte Johnson (January 20, 1929 - July 3, 2019)

Johnson was a comic actor best known for his characters on *Rowan and Martin's Laugh-In.* In live-action, he also appeared in the movies *The Wild and the Innocent, The Third Day, The President's Analyst, Once Upon a Brothers Grimm, Bud and Lou, Love at First Bite, Cannonball Run II, Alice in Wonderland,* and *Evil Spirits.* On TV, he appeared on *The Danny Thomas Show, Hennesey, The Twilight Zone, The Bob Newhart Show, Dr. Kildare, The Andy Griffith Show, McHale's Navy, The Jack Benny Program, Bewitched, The Dick Van Dyke Show, The Donna Reed Show, The Pruitts of Southampton, The Joey Bishop Show, Lost in Space, Hollywood Squares, I Dream of Jeannie, The Andy Williams Show, Sesame Street, The Glen Campbell Goodtime Hour, The David Frost Show,*

*The Dean Marin Show, Night Gallery, The Mike Douglas Show, The Partridge Family, Here's Lucy, Dinah!, The Match Game, Get Christie Love!, The Rookies, Tattletales, The Bobby Vinton Show, The Merv Griffin Show, The Love Boat, Kojak, Fantasy Island, The Dukes of Hazzard, Fame, Hotel, Trapper John MD, Airwolf, The A Team, The New Mike Hammer, Murder She Wrote, Night Court, Parker Lewis Can't Lose,* and *Mad About You.* For voice acting, he appeared on *The Super 6, The Pink Panther Show, The Houndcats, Baggy Pants and the Nitwits, The Dukes, The Smurfs, Foofer, The Flintstone Kids, DuckTales, Snorks, Fantastic Max, The Further Adventures of SuperTed, Tom & Jerry Kids, Yo Yogi!, SWAT Kats, Animaniacs, Sylvester & Tweety Mysteries,* and *Justice League Unlimited.*

## Paul Kirby (details not available)

Kirby was a voice actor and a writer who did voices for *The Richie Rich/Scooby-Doo Show, The Dukes, Snorks, Pole Position*, and as a live-action actor on *Walker Texas Ranger.*

## Chris Latta (August 30, 1949 - June 12, 1994)

Latta was also known as Christopher Collins. He was a film actor, voice actor and comedian. His best known roles were of Cobra Commander on *G.I. Joe*, Starscream in *The Transformers* and the first voice of Moe Szyslak and Mr. Burns for *The Simpsons*. He died of a cerebral hemorrhage at the age of 44. As a voice actor, he also appeared in *Star Blazers, Spider-Man and his Amazing Friends, Inspector Gadget, Inhumanoids, Visionaries, Superman, This is America Charlie Brown,* and *The Real Ghostbusters,* and in live-action *Mr. Belvedere, Mama's Family, Star Trek: The Next Generation, Doogie Howser MD, Seinfeld, The Golden Palace, NYPD Blue, Star Trek: Deep Space Nine,* and *Married with Children.*

Kris Erik Stevens (details not available) Stevens was a radio personality, actor and voice actor. He voiced for *Scooby-Doo and Scrappy-Doo, Richie Rich, The Smurfs* and appeared in *Roseanne, China Beach* and *Human Giant.*

## Andre Stojka (May 26, 1944 - )

Stojka was an actor, singer and voice actor. He is best known as the voice of Owl in the *Winnie the Pooh* series replacing Hal Smith. He also did voices for *Scooby-Doo and Scrappy-Doo, Richie Rich, Shirt Tales, ABC Weekend Specials, Pink Panther and Sons, Challenge of the GoBots, The Jetsons, Rainbow Brite, Wildfire, Jonny Quest, Superman, Yogi's Treasure Hunt, Bobby's World, Adventures of* the Gummi Bears, Fantastic Max, The Pirates of Dark Water, SWAT Kats, Men in Black, Darkwing Duck, House of Mouse, Cow and Chicken, and The Grim Adventures of Billy & Mandy.

## Janet Waldo (February 4, 1920 - June 12, 2016)

Waldo was a radio, film and voice actress best known for the roles of Judy Jetson, Penelope Pitstop and Josie from *Josie and the Pussycats*. On radio, she was the lead role in *Meet Corliss Archer* and also was a regular on *The Gallant Heart, Lady of the Press, The Adventures of Ozzie and Harriet, The Eddie Bracken Show, People are Funny, The Fabulous Dr. Tweedy,* and *Young Love*. On TV, she appeared on *I Love Lucy, The Phil Silvers Show, The Lucy Show, The Andy Griffith Show, Please Don't Eat the Daisies, Get Smart, The FBI, Petticoat Junction, Julia,* and a number of uncredited parts in older movies. For voicework, she was on *The Flintstones, The Magilla Gorilla Show, Jonny Quest, Peter Potamus, The Atom Ant/Secret Squirrel Show, Laurel and Hardy, Space Kidettes, The Adventures of Superboy, Space Ghost and Dino Boy, Shazzan, The New Adventures of Huckleberry Finn, Wacky Races, Jack and the Beanstalk, The Fantastic Four, Help It's the Hair Bear Bunch, The Funky Phantom, The Amazing Chan and the Chan Clan, The Roman Holidays, Around the World in 80 Days, Speed Buggy, Inch High Private Eye, The Addams Family, The New Scooby Doo Movies, Jeannie, Hong Kong Phooey, These are the Days, The Tiny Tree, Jabberjaw, CB Bears, Captain Caveman and the Teen Angels, Galaxy Goof-Ups, Battle of the Planets, The New Fred and Barney Show, The Super Globetrotters, Scooby-Doo and Scrappy-Doo, The All-New Popeye Hour, Thundarr the Barbarian, Spider-Man and his Amazing Friends, The Smurfs, The Puppy's Further Adventures, Alvin and the Chipmunks, The Dukes, Rubik the Amazing Cube, Mr. T, Yogi's Treasure Hunt, Wake Rattle and Roll, Tom & Jerry Kids, Droopy: Master Detective,* and *King of the Hill*.

## THE CREW:

### Directed by

George Gordon: (21 episodes, 1982-1983)
Ray Patterson: (21 episodes, 1982-1983)
Carl Urbano: (21 episodes, 1982-1983)
Rudy Zamora: (21 episodes, 1982-1983)
Bob Hathcock: (13 episodes, 1982)
Bill Hutten: (13 episodes, 1982)
Oscar Dufau: (8 episodes, 1983)
John Walker: (8 episodes, 1983)

### Written by

Don Dougherty: (8 episodes, 1983)
Toru Iwatani: (uncredited) (unknown episodes)
Jeffrey Scott: (20 episodes, 1982-1983)

### Produced by

Joseph Barbera: executive producer (21 episodes, 1982-1983)
William Hanna: executive producer (21 episodes, 1982-1983)
Iwao Takamoto: creative producer (21 episodes, 1982-1983)
Kay Wright: producer (21 episodes, 1982-1983)

### Developed for television by

Jeffrey Scott: (21 episodes, 1982-1983)

### Music

Hoyt Curtin: (21 episodes, 1982-1983)

## Film Editing

Gil Iverson: (21 episodes, 1982-1983)

## Casting

Ginny McSwain: (21 episodes, 1982-1983)

## Production Management

Jayne Barbera: executive in charge of production (21 episodes, 1982-1983)
Joed Eaton: post-production supervisor (21 episodes, 1982-1983)
Margaret Loesch: executive in charge of production / supervising executive (21 episodes, 1982-1983)
Peter Aries: production manager (8 episodes, 1983)
Jean MacCurdy: executive in charge of production (8 episodes, 1983)

## Second Unit Director or Assistant Director

Bob Goe: assistant director (21 episodes, 1982-1983)
Terence Harrison: assistant director (13 episodes, 1982)
Bill Hutten: assistant director (8 episodes, 1983)
Tony Love: (8 episodes, 1983)
Don Lusk: (8 episodes, 1983)
Ann Tucker: (8 episodes, 1983)

## Art Department

Iraj Paran: graphics (21 episodes, 1982-1983)
Mitch Schauer: story director (21 episodes, 1982-1983)
Bob Singer: design supervisor (21 episodes, 1982-1983)
Roy Wilson: story director (21 episodes, 1982-1983)
Tom Wogatzke: graphics (21 episodes, 1982-1983)
Steve Hickner: story director (13 episodes, 1982)
Tom Tataranowicz: story director (13 episodes, 1982)
Wendell Washer: story director (13 episodes, 1982)
Ron Campbell: story director (8 episodes, 1983)

Gary Hoffman: story director (8 episodes, 1983)
Larry Latham: story director (8 episodes, 1983)
Kay Wright: story director (8 episodes, 1983)

## Sound Department

Pat Foley: dubbing supervisor (21 episodes, 1982-1983)
Gordon Hunt: recording director (21 episodes, 1982-1983)
Michael Bradley: sound effects editor (13 episodes, 1982)
Mary Gleason: sound effects editor (13 episodes, 1982)
Carol Lewis: sound effects editor (13 episodes, 1982)
Catherins MacKenzie: sound effects editor (13 episodes, 1982)
Richard Olson: sound director (13 episodes, 1982)
Sue Sawade: sound effects editor (13 episodes, 1982)
Joe Wachter: sound director (13 episodes, 1982)
Kerry Dean Williams: sound effects editor (13 episodes, 1982)
Robert Belcher: sound effects editor (8 episodes, 1983)
Alvy Dorman: sound director (8 episodes, 1983)
Phil Flad: sound director (8 episodes, 1983)
William R. Kowalchuk Jr.: sound effects editor (8 episodes, 1983)

## Camera and Electrical Department

Steve Altman: camera operator (13 episodes, 1982)
Charles Flekal: camera operator (13 episodes, 1982)
Curt Hall: camera operator (13 episodes, 1982)
Ralph Migliori: camera operator (13 episodes, 1982)
Joe A. Ponticelle: camera operator (13 episodes, 1982)
David Valentine: camera operator (13 episodes, 1982)
Roy Wade: camera operator (13 episodes, 1982)
Jerry Whittington: camera operator (13 episodes, 1982)
Bob Cohen: camera operator (8 episodes, 1983)
Bob Marples: camera operator (8 episodes, 1983)

## Animation Department

Fernando Arce: background artist (21 episodes, 1982-1983)
Bonnie Callahan: background artist (21 episodes, 1982-1983)

Jaime Diaz: layout artist / animation supervisor / layout supervisor (21 episodes, 1982-1983)
Martin Forte: background artist (21 episodes, 1982-1983)
Robert Gentle: background artist (21 episodes, 1982-1983)
Al Gmuer: background supervisor (21 episodes, 1982-1983)
Phil Lewis: background artist (21 episodes, 1982-1983)
Lorraine Marue: background artist (21 episodes, 1982-1983)
Andrew Phillipson: background artist (21 episodes, 1982-1983)
Bill Proctor: background artist (21 episodes, 1982-1983)
Ron Roesch: background artist (21 episodes, 1982-1983)
Gloria Wood: background artist (21 episodes, 1982-1983)
Sue Adnopoz: layout artist (13 episodes, 1982)
Robert Alvarez: animator (13 episodes, 1982)
Kurt Anderson: layout artist (13 episodes, 1982)
Cosmo Anzilotti: layout artist (13 episodes, 1982)
Monique Barreras: animator (13 episodes, 1982)
Rex Barron: layout artist (13 episodes, 1982)
Bob Bemiller: animator (13 episodes, 1982)
Sandra Berez: character designer (13 episodes, 1982)
Barrington Bunce: layout artist (13 episodes, 1982)
Oliver Callahan: animator (13 episodes, 1982)
Rudy Cataldi: animator (13 episodes, 1982)
Gary Conklin: background artist (13 episodes, 1982)
Tom Coppola: layout artist (13 episodes, 1982)
Franco Cristofani: layout artist (13 episodes, 1982)
Zeon Davush: animator (13 episodes, 1982)
Gil DiCicco: background artist (13 episodes, 1982)
Barbara Dourmaskin-Case: layout artist (13 episodes, 1982)
Joan Drake: animator (13 episodes, 1982)
Dave Dunnet: layout artist (13 episodes, 1982)
Jon Elford: animator (13 episodes, 1982)
Lillian Evans: animator (13 episodes, 1982)
Flamarion Ferreira: background artist (13 episodes, 1982)
Owen Fitzgerald: layout artist (13 episodes, 1982)
Hugh Fraser: animator (13 episodes, 1982)
Andrew Gentle: layout artist (13 episodes, 1982)
Valerie Gifford: animator (13 episodes, 1982)
Mo Gollub: layout artist (13 episodes, 1982)
Carol Holman Grosvenor: layout artist (13 episodes, 1982)
Charles Grosvenor: layout artist (13 episodes, 1982)
Paul Gruwell: layout artist (13 episodes, 1982)
Jeff Hall: animator (13 episodes, 1982)
Bob Hathcock: animator (13 episodes, 1982)

Deborah Hayes: character designer (13 episodes, 1982)
Fred Hellmich: animator (13 episodes, 1982)
Wes Herschensohn: layout artist (13 episodes, 1982)
Eric Heschong: background artist (13 episodes, 1982)
Jim Hickey: background artist (13 episodes, 1982)
David Hilberman: layout artist (13 episodes, 1982)
Gary Hoffman: layout supervisor (13 episodes, 1982)
John Howley: layout artist (13 episodes, 1982)
Paro Hozumi: background artist (13 episodes, 1982)
Terry Hudson: layout artist (13 episodes, 1982)
Michael Humphries: background artist (13 episodes, 1982)
Bill Hutten: animator (13 episodes, 1982)
Raymond Jacobs: layout artist (13 episodes, 1982)
Vicky Jenson: background artist (13 episodes, 1982)
Mary Jorgensen: layout artist (13 episodes, 1982)
Karenia Kaminski: layout artist (13 episodes, 1982)
Karen Kastelman: animator (13 episodes, 1982)
Mike Kawaguchi: layout artist (13 episodes, 1982)
John Kricfaluci: layout artist (13 episodes, 1982)
Ken Landau: layout artist (13 episodes, 1982)
Alison Leopold: ink and paint supervisor (13 episodes, 1982)
Lonnie Lloyd: layout artist (13 episodes, 1982)
Hicks Lokey: animator (13 episodes, 1982)
Tony Love: animator (13 episodes, 1982)
Michael Maliani: layout artist (13 episodes, 1982)
Jack Manning: layout artist (13 episodes, 1982)
Mircea Mantta: animator (13 episodes, 1982)
Warren Marshall: layout artist (13 episodes, 1982)
Greg Martin: layout artist (13 episodes, 1982)
Lorenzo Martinez: layout artist (13 episodes, 1982)
Alex McCrae: layout artist (13 episodes, 1982)
Darrell McNeil: layout artist (13 episodes, 1982)
Marija Miletic Dail: layout artist (13 episodes, 1982)
Skip Morgan: layout artist (13 episodes, 1982)
Jim Mueller: layout artist (13 episodes, 1982)
Terry Lee Mullen: layout artist (13 episodes, 1982)
Kenneth Muse: animator (13 episodes, 1982)
Constantin Mustatea: animator (13 episodes, 1982)
Ron Myrick: animator (13 episodes, 1982)
Bob Nesler: animator (13 episodes, 1982)
Margaret Nichols: animator (13 episodes, 1982)
Judith Niver: layout artist (13 episodes, 1982)
Floyd Norman: layout artist (13 episodes, 1982)

Bill Nunes: animator (13 episodes, 1982)
David O'Day: layout artist (13 episodes, 1982)
Michael O'Mara: layout artist (13 episodes, 1982)
Phil Ortiz: layout artist (13 episodes, 1982)
John Perry: layout artist (13 episodes, 1982)
Philip Phillipson: background artist / layout artist (13 episodes, 1982)
Mario Piluso: layout artist (13 episodes, 1982)
Barney Posner: animator (13 episodes, 1982)
Bill Pratt: animator (13 episodes, 1982)
Jeff Richards: background artist (13 episodes, 1982)
Jeff Riche: background artist (13 episodes, 1982)
Joanna Romersa: assistant animation supervisor (13 episodes, 1982)
Darrell Rooney: layout artist (13 episodes, 1982)
Linda Rowley: layout artist (13 episodes, 1982)
Don Ruch: animator (13 episodes, 1982)
Jay Sarbry: animation supervisor (13 episodes, 1982)
Joel Siebel: layout artist (13 episodes, 1982)
Kunio Shimamura: animator (13 episodes, 1982)
Michael Silbereich: animator (13 episodes, 1982)
Jim Simon: animator / layout artist (13 episodes, 1982)
Bob Smith: layout artist (13 episodes, 1982)
Ken Southworth: animator (13 episodes, 1982)
Bob C. Strickland: checking and scene planning (13 episodes, 1982)
Leo D. Sullivan: layout artist (13 episodes, 1982)
Takashi: character designer (13 episodes, 1982)
Gary Terry: layout artist (13 episodes, 1982)
Dean Thompson: layout artist (13 episodes, 1982)
Maureen Trueblood: layout artist (13 episodes, 1982)
Richard Trueblood: animator (13 episodes, 1982)
Bob Tyler: layout artist (13 episodes, 1982)
Peter Van Elk: background artist (13 episodes, 1982)
Dennis Venizelos: background artist (13 episodes, 1982)
James T. Walker: animator (13 episodes, 1983)
Sherilan Weinhart: layout artist (13 episodes, 1982)
David West: layout artist (13 episodes, 1982)
Dave Williams: layout artist (13 episodes, 1982)
Roy Wilson: layout artist (13 episodes, 1982)
Star Wirth: xeroxographer (13 episodes, 1982)
Woody Yocum: animator (13 episodes, 1983)
Michele Moen: background artist (12 episodes, 1982)
Susan Beak: animator (8 episodes, 1983)
Roger Chiasson: animation supervisor (8 episodes, 1983)
Geofrey Darrow: character designer (8 episodes, 1983)

Davis Doi: character designer (8 episodes, 1983)
Dick Dunn: animator (8 episodes, 1983)
Peter Gardiner: animator (8 episodes, 1983)
Jonathon E. Goloy: background artist (8 episodes, 1983)
Gerry Grabner: animator (8 episodes, 1983)
Greg Ingram: animator (8 episodes, 1983)
Paul Maron: animator (8 episodes, 1983)
Jon McClenahan: animator (8 episodes, 1983)
Busina Milan: layout artist (8 episodes, 1983)
Chris Minos: layout artist (8 episodes, 1983)
Sean Newton: animation supervisor (8 episodes, 1983)
Chris Otsuki: character designer (8 episodes, 1983)
Don Patterson: animation supervisor (8 episodes, 1983)
Bruce Pederson: layout artist (8 episodes, 1983)
Joe Shearer: layout artist (8 episodes, 1983)
Peter Sheehan: layout artist (8 episodes, 1983)
Richard Slapcynski: layout artist (8 episodes, 1983)
Don Spencer: animation supervisor (8 episodes, 1983)
Mike Stapleton: animator (8 episodes, 1983)
Jim Stenstrum: character designer (8 episodes, 1983)
Michael Takamoto: character designer (8 episodes, 1983)
Pere Van Reyk: layout artist (8 episodes, 1983)
Adriana Cerrotti: assistant animator (uncredited) (unknown episodes)
Néstor Córdoba: animator (uncredited) (unknown episodes)

## Editorial Department

Larry C. Cowan: supervising film editor (21 episodes, 1982-1983)
William E. DeBoer: negative consultant (21 episodes, 1982-1983)

## Music Department

Hoyt Curtin: musical director (21 episodes, 1982-1983)
Paul DeKorte: music supervisor (21 episodes, 1982-1983)
Terry Moore: music editor (13 episodes, 1982)
Joe Sandusky: music editor (13 episodes, 1982)
Robert Talboy: music editor (13 episodes, 1982)

## Additional Crew

Donald Loughery: creative consultant (21 episodes, 1982-1983)
Jerry Mills: technical supervisor (13 episodes, 1982)
Bill Perez: title designer (8 episodes, 1983)
Robin Strickland: production assistant (8 episodes, 1983)
James Wang: production coordinator (8 episodes, 1983)

# Pac-Man Episode Guide

Season one (1982-1983) as part of *The Pac-Man/Little Rascals/Richie Rich Show*:

The opening on all episodes show Pac-Man fleeing the ghost monsters (Inky, Blinky, Pinky, Clyde and Sue) until he eats some power pellets and then starts chomping ghosts. The standard Pac-Man theme song plays in the background and a deep-voiced person announces "Pac-Man". Pac-man responds, "That's me!" as the ghost eyes float away. The entire Pac-family of Pac-Man, Pepper, Pac-Baby, Chomp-Chomp and Sour Puss is then shown on Mezmaron's TV who shouts, "Oh, I must have those power pellets! Go find me the Power Pellet Forest!" to the ghost eyes that have now shown up in his lair. The eyes put on new ghost suits and are ready to get Pac-Man and Pepper again. This time Pac-Baby powers up and chases the ghosts that are chasing his parents. The title "Pac-Man" is revealed with the standard Hanna-Barbera orchestral crash.

1. Presidential Pac-Nappers (September 25, 1982) Story by Jeffrey Scott

It's a regular day in Pac-Land. Pac-Man flees the ghost monsters and needs some power pellets as his energy is getting low. The chase continues. A pipe is set up to capture Pac-Man, but instead it hurls him up in the air and he crashes down. Pac-Man makes it home and wife Pepper Pac-Man saves the day by feeding Pac-Man a good supply of power pellets and now the tables are turned and Pac eats the ghosts with Ms. Pac's help. The ghosts turn invisible and they run to Mezmaron's lab to be reinstated with new ghost suits. Mezmaron has a new plan for the ghosts, to get the Pac-President, in order to get Pac-Man, as Pac will come to the President's rescue. The ghosts Pac-nap the President and make a broadcast on TV alerting Pac-Man. While the ghosts, they take over the Pac-House. Pac-Man arrives and is chased by the ghosts. Pac-Man escapes the ghosts, releases Pac-President from his cage and feeds him his last Pac-Pellet. The ghosts take over again and want to know where the Power Forest is. Pac-Man gives in and tells that it is on the other side of the forest, but Pac-Man has misled him to a different spot and multiple Pac-Men eat Mezmaron. Ms. Pac-Man arrives with a picnic basket of Pac-Pellets and Mr. and Ms. start chomping ghosts. One stray ghost hides in the water, but he is chomped, too, and in the end the Pac-couple eat more power pellets as Mezmaron is chased out of town by the other chomping Pacs.

Pac-Mania bumper: Pac-Man is running from the ghosts and is out of power pellets. He only has some instant growth cactus seeds in his pocket which he plants. The quickly grown cactus spears the ghosts and Pac-Man gets away.

2. Picnic in Pacland (September 25, 1982) Story by Jeffrey Scott

Another busy day on the Pac-freeway as everyone is speeding in their Pac-Cars. The Pac-Man families go to Pacland Park. People are relaxing while Pepper sets up a picnic blanket and a barbecue grill. Later, the Ms. grills some power pellet burgers, but until they're ready, Pac-Man plays disc toss with Chomp-Chomp the dog. Sour Puss the cat makes Chomp-Chomp chase a disc up a tree so he can cut the branch and make him fall, but Chomp-Chomp escapes. Meanwhile, the ghosts are also relaxing in Pac-Land Park. The disc flies into the ghosts' picnic and they get the bright idea to meld into a ghost disc to have Chomp-Chomp bring them back to Pac-Man. Chomp-Chomp buries the ghost disc instead. Pac-Man and Chomp-Chomp go back to their picnic and Chomp-Chomp tries to eat Pac-Man's Pac-burger. The ghosts try to upset Pac-Man's picnic with Pac-ants, but they get chomped instead. After eating, the Pac family go fishing on their boat. Pac-Man catches a fish which lands in Chomp-Chomp's mouth and it comes out bones. Sour Puss tries to catch a fish with Pac-worms. The ghosts now don swimming masks and pretend to be a shark to scare Pac-Man, but they are soon chomped by a real Pac-shark. The ghosts come back to pull on Pac-Man's fishing line as the Pac-worm flees. Pac-Man ends up pulling up the Pac-shark. Later, the Pacs with Pac-Baby play Pac-chess, fly a Pac-kite and the ghosts try yet again to disrupt their fun by becoming a ghost kite, but this plan backfires, too, as they get struck by lightning. It's time for the Pac-family to go home and they get in their car and leave. The ghosts are left behind nursing their bruised and bandaged ghost bodies.

3. The Great Pac-Quake (October 2, 1982) Story by Jeffrey Scott

Pac-Man is delivered a package that is supposedly top secret. It turns out to be a box of ghosts. Pac-Man is in the Pac Forest and now the ghosts know where the source of the power pellets is. Pac-Man gets low on Pac-energy, but eats a bunch of power pellets and chases the ghosts, who hide in a tent. Too late, as Pac-Man eats them and the eyes flee to Mezmaron's lair. Mezmaron commands the ghosts to get into their new suits. The ghosts tell Mezmaron that they know where the power forest is, but no one remembers how they got there. Now, Mezmaron gives the ghosts a transmitter to make a Pac-quake and they start an earthquake in Pac-Land in order for the ghosts to steal the secret map of Pac-Land held in the Pac-museum. They succeed in getting the map. Sue wants to get the map to Mezmaron, but the other ghosts just want to use the map to go to the forest. Unfortunately, none of the ghosts really know how to read a map. Pac-Man sees what the ghosts are up to and dons a beard for a disguise to lead the ghosts down the wrong road. The ghosts escape and try again in a helicopter which gets chomped. Pac-parrot tells Pac-Man to switch the Pac-Land maps on the ghosts. With the new map, the ghosts turn on the quaking device again to get the power pellets to shake off the trees, but due to the bad map, shakes Mezmeron's lair instead. Pac-Man powers up again and gets the ghosts one last time. He now needs rest, but accidentally sits on the quaking machine.

Pac-Mania bumper: The ghosts chase Pac-Man once again. Pac-Man paints a cave on the wall to escape through. He escapes, but the ghosts do not, becoming invisible eyes after they crash into the wall.

4. Hocus-Pocus Pac-Man (October 2, 1982) Story by Jeffrey Scott

The Pac-family gets some Pac-mail delivered by the Pac-postman. Pac-Man relaxes in a hammock. Soon, Chomp-Chomp and Sour Puss disrupt Pac-Man's sleep. Pac-Man fixes his hammock and goes back to sleep. Pepper then tells Pac-Man to watch Pac-Baby as he sleeps, but Pac-Man gets no sleep. Pac-Man puts Pac-Baby in a Pac-pen so he can sleep, but he escapes and starts driving the Pac-mower. Of course, Pac-Man still gets no sleep. Pac-man puts Pac-Baby back in his overturned Pac-pen so he won't escape, but Pac-Baby eats some power pellets and escapes anyway and starts chomping everything in sight. Pac-Man chases after him to try to get him back home. Pac-Man decides to read Pac-Baby a story after they get back home. He teaches him about Pac-magic, which amuses Pac-Baby, as he performs some ball and card tricks. Next he does a Pac-rabbit

out of the hat trick. In the process, he accidentally makes Pac-Baby disappear in the hat. Pepper calls home to check to see if everything is ok and Pac-Man hangs up on her. Meanwhile, Chomp-Chomp and Sour Puss get into other mischief with the washing machine with the expected results of a soaked cat. Pac-Man is still looking for Pac-Baby as Pepper returns home with groceries. Pac-Man puts Chomp-Chomp in the Pac-crib to fool Pepper, but Pepper figures out the ruse. Pac-Man comes clean and explains how he lost Pac-Baby. In doing so, he says the magic words and Pac-Baby returns, to everyone's relief. Pac-Man then tries to relax one more time, but gets trampled on by Chomp-Chomp and Sour Puss.

5. Southpaw Packy (October 9, 1982) Story by Jeffrey Scott

The Pac-family is taking another drive, this time to the Pac-Land World Series. While Pac-Man drives, Chomp-Chomp chases Sour Puss around the car, causing Pac-Man to drive onto a Pac-officer's motorcycle. After a few tickets, Pac-Man finally gets to the World Series. An announcer introduces The Pacsburg Pickers playing the Pelletstown Chompers and calls the plays, until the ghosts come in and interfere with the gameplay. Pac-Man and family won't let the ghosts ruin the World Series. The ghosts challenge Pac-Man to a baseball game and so their game begins. Pac-Man hits a home run as his family cheer him on. After running, Pac-Man runs out of energy. Pepper is up next and she also hits the ball, but Chomp-Chomp chases the ball and gives it to a ghost and Pepper is tagged out. Chomp-Chomp makes amends by hitting a single. Sour Puss is up next, but she is up to mischief again by installing a spring-loaded base, which ultimately backfires. Now the ghosts are up to bat and, of course, they cheat when they play. In the ninth inning, the ghosts are ahead by a run. Pac-Man is up at bat again and the ghosts plot to attack him. Pac-Man eats some emergency pellets in order to eat the cheating ghosts. They succeed and the ghost eyes flee. With the ghosts now gone, the Pac-family easily wins. The announcer comes out to congratulate the family.

Pac-Mania bumper: Sour Puss tries to disturb Chomp-Chomp's sleep by setting him on top of a ladder so she can push him into some garbage. Sour Puss swings on a rope and misses Chomp-Chomp, landing in the garbage instead.

6. Pac-Baby Panic (October 9, 1982) Story by Jeffrey Scott

Pepper asks Pac-Man what he's hiding under the bed. It is power pellet seeds. Soon, Baby-Pac discovers them and the ghosts also arrive to find them, too. They find the sack under the bed. Pac-Man bursts in to catch them, but the ghosts have the upper hand because they have the power pellets. Soon, a high-speed chase occurs where the ghosts chase Pac-Man at top speed. Pac is defeated so Pepper gives him Packies: the Breakfast of Chompions and he gets the ghosts. Ghost Sue tries to disguise herself as clothes on a line, but gets chomped by Pepper. Pac-Man is happy, but it is short-lived as he realizes the ghosts still have the bag of power pellets. They give the bag to Mezmaron, who is happy. He opens up the bag and discovers Pac-Baby in the bag and decides to make him his hostage. Pac-Man and Pepper are on their way in their car to try to retrieve the power pellets with the restored ghosts in tow. The Pac couple drive through a car wash to rid them of the ghosts. Meanwhile, Mezmaron is having his own problems as Pac-Baby turns out to be a handful, destroying Mezmaron's headquarters. The ghosts try again to capture Pac-Man by pretending to be police officers on a motorcycle. They pull over Pac-Man and Pepper and tell them that Mezmaron has Pac-Baby and their pellets, plus Mezmaron's demands. Mezmaron puts Inky in charge of babysitting and Pac-Baby eats all of the pellets in the bag and becomes super, eating all of the ghosts. He also tries to eat Mezmaron. Pac-Man and Pepper show up and Mezmaron gives Pac-Baby back with no problems as he is a true pain in the neck.

7. Pacula (October 16, 1982) Story by Jeffrey Scott

It's a rainy night and the ghosts are trying to track down the Pac-pellets in a graveyard, but they come across Pac-Man instead. He comes across a grave marked "R.I.P" and concludes it contains reinforcement power pellets, and he is correct. He eats some and chomps the ghosts. One of the ghosts is chomped by a Pac-skeleton who has risen from the grave to chomp him. Back at Mezmaron's lair, the ghosts have returned, but Mezmaron is not happy. He wants to replace the ghosts with a bat. Mezmaron transforms the bat into a vampire named Pacula. Pacula wants to eat the ghosts, but Mezmaron says to eat Pac-Land people instead. Pacula arrives at a drive-through showing Pac-Wars and starts biting various Pac-people. Pacula demands to know the location of the Pac-Forest and begins to chase Pac-Man and Pepper. Pac-Man discovers a power pellet possesses the same powers of a cross on Dracula. Mezmaron is watching everything on his viewscreen and is happy that he will know the location of the Pac-forest soon. The ghosts are now mad that they have been replaced by Pacula. They eat Mezmaron's serum and become ghost-bats or ghost-vampires. Meanwhile, Pac-Man and Pepper are in search of a haunted castle so they can capture Count Pacula. Pacula demands to know the location of the Pac-forest, but soon the ghosts show up wanting their jobs back. Soon, it is morning and the combination of both the sun and the power pellets defeats Pacula as well as the ghosts. Pac-Man and Pepper are happy with their achievement, but Pacula's grave opens again and scares them off.

Pac-Mania bumper: The ghosts are chasing Pac-Man, who jumps into a Pac-manhole. It turns out to be the old painted cave on the wall gag as Pac-Man can jump into and out of the manhole and the ghosts can't, so Pac-Man escapes.

8. Trick or Chomp (October 16, 1982) Story by Jeffrey Scott

Pac-Baby tries to help Pac-Man wash dishes, but they end up breaking more instead. Pepper comes in to say that Pac-Man and Pac-Baby are going trick or treating as it's Pac-Baby's first Halloween. Pac-Man dresses as a cowboy and Pepper and Pac-Baby just wear masks. Pac-Man shows Pac-Baby how to trick or treat and gets terrified in the process. The others including Chomp-Chomp and Sour Puss all get many pac pellet treats. Pac-Man comes back and is told he's too old to be trick or treating. Chomp-Chomp then tries to hide Chomp-Chomp in a Jack-o-Lantern and takes him to the airport to be flown away. The plan backfires as the pumpkin is tossed out of the plane and lands on Sour Puss breaking Chomp-Chomp's fall. The ghosts finally arrive to see all the various Pac-Land people trick or treating. They decide to trick or treat to scare, not to get treats. One ghost blows up like a balloon to scare people, but Chomp-Chomp bites him and he swirls around like a popped balloon. Next, the ghosts wrap themselves up to make a very tall mummy, but their rags get spun off them making them dizzy. Pepper tells Pac-Man and Pac-Baby that they are going to go to one more house and then go home. This last house is haunted and Pac-Man is nervous. The ghosts are waiting in the pipe organ and in paintings to try to scare everyone, but fail. Suddenly, Pac-Baby and then Chomp-Chomp and then Sour Puss go missing. Eventually everyone falls into the ghosts' trap and they fall through the floor to a holding pot. Pac-Man sees failure but Pac-Baby takes out all of his Halloween treats. Everyone eats the ghosts and they shout "Happy Halloween" as the ghosts fly away. .

9.  Super Ghosts (October 23, 1982) Story by Jeffrey Scott

At the crossroads, the ghosts are disguised as lost power pellet trees. A truck comes by to take them back to where they belong. Now, the ghosts will know the location of the power pellet forest. The ghosts actually were taken to the power pellet picking plant thanks to Pac-Man. He sends the ghost trees through the machinery which destroys the ghosts. The ghosts race back to Mezmaron's hideout. Mezmaron is mad at the ghosts for failing again. Mezmaron is working on a special formula, but the ghosts accidentally destroy it, or have they? The formula makes them super ghosts. Mezmaron says that now that the ghosts are super, to go and find the power forest. Pac-Man is alerted that the ghosts are now attacking Pac-Land and terrorizing the Pac people. They ruin the bridge that Pepper is driving on and Pac-Man saves her. Pepper and Pac-Man try to hide from the ghosts but cannot. Sue chomps Pepper and the rest of the ghosts take away Pac-Man's powers. The ghosts want to know where the forest was, but then figure if they have super powers, they no longer have to follow Mezmaron's orders. Pac-Man and Pepper go back home and Pepper whips up a power pellet recipe that makes them more super than the ghosts. As the Super-Pacs, Pac-Man and Pepper defeat the ghosts one at a time. Pac-Man celebrates his success by flying around, but then crashes down to the ground when his power starts running out, prompting Pepper to say, "You're always super to me."
Pac-Mania bumper: Chomp-Chomp is eating a bone. Sour Puss tries to squirt him with a hose, but the water backs up and gets Sour Puss instead.

10. The Pac-Man in the Moon (October 23, 1982) Story by Jeffrey Scott

Pac-Man and Pepper are watching a space shuttle launch. The ghosts have written instructions from Mezmaron including one to not stand too close to the shuttle's engines, which of course, they do. The ghosts reorganize and take

over the Pac-shuttle. Pac-Man is able to take care of the ghosts before they do. Pac-Man needs some reinforcements and eats more Pac-pellets. The ghosts are chomped but head inside the Pac-shuttle and they end up taking it even in their condition. They crash the Pac-shuttle into Mezmaron's headquarters. The ghosts get new outfits and are told by Mezmaron to take his new vacuum machine and suck all of the power pellets to the Moon. The ghosts then take the shuttle to the Moon with the machine. Pac-Man and Pepper get into their own spaceship and chase after them. Space ghosts start chomping Pac-Man's ship and it crashlands on the Moon. Meanwhile, the ghosts try to land their shuttle on the Moon, but they crashland, too. The ghosts chase the Pacs on the Moon as their power pellets are sucked away from them. The ghosts then start sucking the pellets from Earth to the Moon. The Pacs finally get some pellets from the ghosts and start chomping them one by one. They soon take the vacuum machine, put it in reverse and shoot all the power pellets back to Earth. The defeated ghosts once again crashland the shuttle again from the Moon to Mezmaron's lair. .

11. Invasion of the Pac-Pups (October 30, 1982) Story uncredited

It's rush hour in Pac-Land and the Pac-stork is bringing a new baby to town. In the meantime, Pac-Man is wallpapering, but his ladder gets disrupted by Chomp-Chomp. The Pac-stork brings the Pacs a litter of Pac-puppies. The pups surround and scare Sour Puss. Pac-Man goes back to wallpapering. The puppies are a nuisance and mess up Pac-Man's work again. The puppies mess up the pool table, but Pac-Baby is happy with the pups. The puppies tear up Pac-Man's favorite chair. Finally, Pac-Man has had enough and kicks out the pups and Chomp-Chomp. Chomp-Chomp and the puppies play see-saw and now Sour Puss tries to disrupt their fun, which of course, backfires. Chomp-Chomp and the pups do a tug of war and when a pile of power pellets become available courtesy of Sour Puss, the pups eat them and become super and tear more things up. Morris, Pac-Man's neighbor stops by and asks if Pac-Man can help him paint his garage. Pac-Man agrees in order to get away from the Pac-puppies, but the pups and Chomp-Chomp follow them and create more havoc. Pac-Man and Morris try to lure all of the pups out of the house with power pellets. They decide to wait it out as the puppies are still too powerful, but Pepper takes pity on the pups and feeds them again! Pac-Man and Morris keep hiding, but the puppies keep causing more troubles. Finally, they surrender. The Pac-stork returns for the puppies claiming that he delivered them to the wrong address, but then the Pac-stork brings more Pac-kittens.

Pac-Mania bumper: Mezmaron wants more power pellets and sends the ghosts with a spring hand contraption which backfires and flattens the ghosts.

12. Journey to the Center of Pacland (October 30, 1982) Story by Jeffrey Scott

At Pac-Land's department of water, the ghosts are planning to get inside the water tank that takes water to the power pellet forest. At the plant, the Pac-workers divert the water to the Pac-Land Zoo as there has been enough water sent to the forest. At the Zoo, the ghosts are chased by Pac-odiles. The ghosts all get chomped by Pac-Man and return back to Mezmaron. The ghosts get dressed into new clothes. At home, Pac-Man is practicing his juggling. Pac-Man's boss stops by and makes Pac-Man get back to work. The ghosts are back and end up in the forest. Since they suspect the ghosts being there, Pac-Man orders the other workers to hide the power pellet trees and then they eat a number of pellets and Pac-Man leads them military-style to chomp all of the ghosts. Mezmaron is also there in the forest, but the Pac-power troopers chomp Mezmaron and he and all of the ghosts flee back to his lair to get new clothes. Mezmaron wants to go back, but the ghosts ask how to do it without being detected. Mezmaron says they will tunnel underground. They tunnel underneath the forest and start tunneling up, but their calculations turn out to be inaccurate. They actually tunnel underneath the ocean and they get drenched with water. They try again and this time, Mezmaron and the ghosts come up in the middle of town and demand to know the location of the power pellet forest. Pepper says she will tell them, but instead she leads them to a swarm of Pac-hornets. Pac-Man and Pepper power up and chomp the ghosts one by one. The Pacs celebrate their victory until Pac-Man drops into a hole created by so many underground tunnels.

13. The Day the Forest Disappeared (November 6, 1982) Story uncredited

Pac-Man heads off to work. The ghosts are hidden on the hubcaps of his car wheels. As the car rolls, the ghosts get dizzy, muddy and wet and are eventually displaced from the hubcaps. A Pac-bum comes by and eats the ghosts. They go back to Mezmaron and get new ghost suits. His new plan is to use a Pac-pigeon, but the ghosts inadvertently set it free. Meanwhile, Pac-Man is trying to catch a Pac-rat with a net. Just then the boss comes in to chew out Pac-Man for sloppy work. Just then, the ghosts and Mezmaron are following the Pac-pigeon in a hot air balloon. One of the ghosts lets the air out of the balloon too fast and it comes crashing down. Fortunately for them, they landed in the Pac-forest. Pac-Man leads a Pac-army to get the ghosts, but Mezmaron fires a laugh laser gun that makes the entire military crack up. It also makes the ghosts laugh despite Mezmaron telling them that it has no effect on ghosts. Mezmaron and the ghosts inflate the balloon and pull up a few power pellet forests with them. Later, everyone starts laughing and Pac-Man is on his way to get the forest back. With Mezmaron controlling all of the power, there is no electricity in Pac-Land. Pac-Land goes to Mezmaron's lair pretending to be a man from the power company collecting a bill. The ghosts see through the disguise, but Pac-Man gets more power from the forest that Mezmaron has and chomps all the ghosts. Mezmaron feels that he doesn't need the ghosts any more since he has the forest, but Pac-Man points out that the forest is very obedient and follows Pac-Man back to Pac-Land.

Pac-Mania bumper: Sour Puss paints a metal bone white for Chomp-Chomp and uses a magnet to hold him back, but of course it backfires and the magnet traps Sour Puss onto the back of a speeding car.

14. Sir Chomps-a-Lot (November 6, 1982) Story uncredited

There is a traffic jam in Pac-Land due to a power belt inspection station run by ghosts. The ghosts say that the power pellets are diseased and instruct the driver they pulled over to take them to the power forest. There is another road stop run by Pac-Man and the driver stops and explains the situation. The ghosts get out of the car and chase Pac-Man. Pac-Man signals for a power pellet drop and Pac-Man chomps the pellets and then the ghosts. The chomped ghosts fly back to Mezmaron, who is angry at them for bungling again. The ghosts get new clothes and Mezmaron introduces them to his new invention, a time machine. Mezmaron wants to go back in time before Pac-Man hid the power forest. The ghosts go back in time, but too far back, about 1000 years. The ghosts meet up with Sir Chomp-a-Lot, an ancestor of Pac-Man, who is a knight on a horse. Sir Chomps need to be rid of Pac-dragon and the ghosts agree to take care of him in exchange for the Pac-forest. Sir Chomps agrees, but the ghosts are very inept at getting the dragon. The ghosts are tired of this and chase Sir Chomps to a

castle. They try to cross the moat, but encounter a Pac-odile. They finally get into the castle and meet Princess Pac, a princess in a high tower. Sir Chomps-a-Lot challenges the ghosts to a duel. The ghosts have a chomping javelin and defeat Sir Chomps. The castle throws power pellets over the castle walls. Sir Chomps chomps and defeats the ghosts. Sue tries to get Princess Pac, but she gets chomped. Pinky gets chomped by the Pac-dragon and the ghosts and the dragon jump back into the time machine back to Mezmaron's lair. Mezmaron is chased by the dragon in the final scene.

15. Neander-Pac-Man (November 13, 1982) Story by Jeffrey Scott

Police and guns are heard in Pac-Land and Pac-Man can't sleep. Pac-Man gets something out of the fridge; Pac-Man accidentally drops it on the floor and wakes ups Pac-Baby. Pac-Man tries to rock Pac-Baby to sleep, but it doesn't work. Then he tries a story about Pac-Man's ancient caveman ancestors. Neander-Pac-Man is shown painting on a cave wall. Soon there is a volcanic eruption. It turns out to be their Chompasaurus and Saber Puss. Both are much larger than the Pacs. Neander-Pac-Man and family then decide to go hunting. It doesn't work as the pacasaur clobbers Pac-Man. Chompasaurus tries to capture the pacasaur as Saber Puss tries to sabotage his efforts. Saber Puss' nasty ways get her stomped by the pacasaur. Finally, Neander-Pac-Man gets the pacasaur and drags it home. Soon, cave ghost monsters arrive to chomp Neander-Pac-Man, but the ghosts get chomped by the pacasaur. Neander-Pac-Man then makes his most famous discovery - power pellets - but his efforts are thwarted by the reclothed ghosts.

The ghosts chase Neander-Pac-Man through a maze of trees, rocks and bushes. Finally, the power pellets discover Neander-Pac-Man as one falls in his mouth after he smashes into a tree. Neander-Pac-Man then chomps the ghosts. One of the ghosts tries to disguise himself as a pacasaur but he gets chomped anyway. We return to the present day, with Pac-Man asleep, but Pac-Baby is still awake demanding "More story". Pac-Man switches the tables and gets into the crib while Pac-Baby reads stories to him and Pac-Man goes back to sleep.

Pac-Mania bumper: Chomp-Chomp sees a bone in a net and chomps it. Sour Puss captures him and he's flung in the air by a kite. The kite hits a TV antenna, Chomp-Chomp falls down a drainpipe and bumps Sour Puss, sending her off into the air. In the end, Sour Puss is hanging on to the tail of an airplane.

16. Backpackin' Packy (November 13, 1982) Story by Jeffrey Scott

Pac-Man is reading the Daily Pac until Chomp-Chomp bites a hole in it. Pac-Baby is going to go baby backpacking. Pepper gets a phone call and is told that the Baby Scout leader can't make it. Pepper asks Pac-Man if he could do it. He complains that it is his day off, but finally agrees. The Baby Scouts arrive and soon Pac-Man is driving all of them plus Chomp-Chomp and Sour Puss. They go to a fast food restaurant and all of the babies order burgers, fries and drinks. They make a big mess in Pac-Man's car and he makes them clean it up. They finally get to the campsite. Pac-Man says that the babies are worse than a pack of wild animals. Just then Chomp-Chomp and Sour Puss chase each other through the car, to make Pac-Man state, "Almost worse." Pac-Man shows the campers how to set up a tent. His tent fails and he wants to see if the babies can do better. They do and Pac-Man says, "Show offs." Pac-Man takes the babies on a hike and they identify safe and unsafe plants. Pac-Man makes a mistake and soon is scratching himself. The ghosts arrive on the scene as Pac-Man is teaching about survival lessons and he gets caught in his own trap. The babies set up traps and capture the ghosts. Pac-Man takes the babies river rafting. The ghosts escape the traps and they go river-rafter with Pinky becoming a raft. The ghosts chase the troop, but helium saves the day. The troops' boat floats on air and the ghosts go over a waterfall. Now it is dark and at the campfire, Pac-Man tells the babies a scary story about a bear. The ghosts arrive again and decide to scare the babies with a bearskin. Pac-Man rushes the babies into their tents. The babies take power pellets and they chomp the ghosts. With the ghosts gone, the babies get into the bearskin and scare Pac-Man who runs off.

17. The Abominable Pac-Man (November 20, 1982) Story uncredited

It's another busy day in Pac-Land as a UFO lands in the middle of town. The ghosts arrive dressed as space aliens. They demand to be taken to the power forest. Pac-Man takes them to the forest. The ghosts take off their disguises and Pac-Man reveals that he has taken them to a projection of the forest. He eats power pellets and chomps the ghosts. The ghosts go back to Mezmaron's lair to get new clothes. After getting angry at the ghosts, he tells the ghosts he has found a new source of power pellets, in the frozen Arctic. Pac-Man is now at work and gets in trouble from the boss for fooling around. The boss gives Pac-Man instructions to get the power forest that's in the frozen north. Pac-Man and Pepper arrive on skis being chased by the ghosts and Mezmaron on skis. The ghosts find a tree and shake it, but they are not rained on by power pellets, they are rained on by snowballs. Pac-Man and Pepper still haven't found anything as the ghosts roll a giant snowball after them. They avoid the snowball which ricochets back and lands on the ghosts and Mezmaron. The ghosts escape and drill large holes in the ice. Pac-Man and Pepper ski onto the ice, but they don't fall into the hole, the rest of the lake falls in taking the ghosts and Mezmaron with them. Next, Pac-Man and Pepper encounter the Abominable Pac-Man who all get caught up in a giant snowball. After they all fall off a cliff, they discover the Pac-forest. All three eat power pellets and chomp the ghosts. The Abominable Pac-Man chases Mezmaron in the final scenes.

Pac-Mania bumper: The ghosts spread jam on the road so they can follow Pac-Man's footprints as he goes to the forest. In their excitement, the ghosts get knotted together and Pac-Man says that now they are in a real jam!

18. The Bionic Pac-Woman (November 20, 1982) Story uncredited

Pac-Man and Pepper are eating at Chelsea's. They order some Wakka Wakka Burgers and Pac-Colas. They eat and Pac-Man needs to go back to work, but are encountered by the ghosts in disguise who want to make a film. The film camera has a red beam that renders Pepper powerless and sucks her into the film. Pac-Man flees until he finds a power pellet gumball machine, eats some and starts chomping the ghosts despite hiding in a Pac-mailbox and Pac-phone booth. The ghosts return to an angry Mezmaron who upset him as they didn't bring back the camera. They did, however, bring back the film which has Pepper embedded in it. Mezmaron introduces Pepper's bionic double designed to replace the real Pepper. Pac-Man wonders where Pepper has been when she finally shows up, at least her double does. Pac-Man is then treated like a basketball by Pepper and he is thrown down a tall chimney. Pac-Man brushes himself off and bionic Pepper apologizes. Pepper wants to go to the forest and Pac-Man drives her. The ghosts follow. Pac-Man drives up Pac's Peak and the ghosts are no longer able to follow as it is so steep. They get to the forest and bionic Pepper reveals that she is going to tell Mezmaron where the forest is. Pac-Man places Pepper under arrest, but she hurls him due to her bionic strength. Pac-Man eats some power pellets and puts bionic Pepper out of commission, so he dresses up like her to fool Mezmaron. Pac-Man as bionic Pepper wants to see the real Pepper on film. Mezmaron obliges and soon Pac-Man reveals himself and gives Pepper some power pellets and together they chomp ghosts as she is finally able to escape the film trap.

19. Chomp-Out at the O.K. Corral (November 27, 1982)

The Pacs take a trip out in the desert. Unfortunately, they may stay longer than they like as they are running out of gas. Pac-Man decides to take a turn to a ghost town because of Pac-Baby's crying. Meanwhile, the ghosts have a child ghost named Dinky along with them who is not having fun. The other ghosts figure the ghost town might be a good place to take him again. Pac-Man, meanwhile, wonders if this is the town where Wyatt Pac-Earp had the shoot-out at the O.K. Corral. He dons a cowboy hat and tries to ride a Pac-horse which bucks him and he hits some Pac-cactus. The ghosts wonder why they don't see any ghosts in the ghost town. One of the others says, "What do you think we are?" Dinky is still not happy and is demanding an ice cream cone. Pac-Man, Pepper and Pac-Baby go into a saloon, which is where all the ghosts are as well. The ghosts slop up their drinks and Pepper goes to eat power pellets, but Sue grabs them before she can. Dinky tries to scare Pac-Baby but gets chomped. Pac-Man and Pepper are now on the hunt for Pac pellets and discover an abandoned bank that has millions of dollars in the vault. They disguise themselves with some empty money bags in order to escape the ghosts. With no car, they discover an abandoned train that still works. The ghosts find a train as well and chase them. Pac-Man's train now runs out of gas and the only thing left to do is to have a Chomp-Out with the ghosts. Dinky is still demanding an ice cream

cone. Pac-Baby comes up with one and Dinky gives him a bag of power pellets for it. Now the chomping of ghosts begins. In the end, Dinky (who is not chomped) and Pac-Baby are now friends and plan to go to the beach.

Pac-Mania bumper: Pac-Man is running from the ghosts, but he quickly paints a new background to the scene of a cattle crossing. The ghosts don't believe it, but get run over by a stampede of cows.

    20. Once Upon a Chomp (November 27, 1982) Story by Jeffrey Scott

    The ghosts are hanging out in a hideout and a fairy ghostmother appears. They make a wish of getting Pac-Man. The ghostmother gives them a book of Mother Ghost rhymes that if read aloud will come true. Meanwhile, Pac-Man is playing golf, but is having trouble as Chomp-Chomp and Pac-Baby eat his pellet balls. Pac-Man tries again with a radio-controlled pellet which bypasses Chomp-Chomp, Pac-Baby and Sour Puss to make a hole-in-one. Pepper asks Pac-Man to run to the store and get some power pellets. The ghosts begin to read a fairy tale out of the book and soon a disguised ghost is offering Pac-Man some power pellet beans and brings them home. Pepper is disappointed and so Pac-Man plants the beans, which creates a huge beanstalk. Pepper still would like some power pellets for her recipe and she and Pac-Man climb the huge stalk. At the top, they come to a huge castle of a giant ghost of Pinky who starts chasing them. Pac-Man and Pepper manage to escape, but not for long, and soon they are trapped in a cage. Pepper says to the ghosts that they haven't finished reading the story and missed the part about the Pac-hen who lays the golden pellets. Pac-Man manages to hurl an apple on the other end of the spoon holding the golden pellets and the pellets fly up to the Pacs in the cage. They immediately eat pellets and start chomping ghosts. Giant Pinky says the Pacs are too small to chomp him. The Pacs flee down the stalk and at the bottom Pepper instructs everyone to start chomping the beanstalk, which falls. The fairy ghostmother shows up and asks the ghosts how the story went and they start chasing her.

    21. The Pac-Love-Boat (December 4, 1982) Story uncredited

    Pac-Man and Pepper wave goodbye from the deck of a ship to Pac-Baby, Chomp-Chomp, Sour Puss and the babysitter. The Pacs are taking a cruise. The ghosts are on the cruise, too. At the last moment, a steward sees a stray box which Pac-Baby, Chomp-Chomp and Sour Puss have climbed into when they ran away from the babysitter. Meanwhile, Pac-Man and Pepper lay out on the sun deck, but it's hot, so Pac-Man gets an umbrella, which turns out to be a ghost umbrella. Before the ghosts can do anything, a gust of wind blows the umbrella from the ship and into the blowhole of a whale. The angry whale chomps him. Still sunbathing, Pac-Man announces that he's going to go for a swim. The reinvigorated ghosts come back to try to get Pac-Man in the pool, but once again are forced overboard. The ghosts don't give up and soon they're back on board and pre-score the diving board so it will break off, but when Pac-Man jumps off of it, nothing happens. The ghosts try and the board fails. Next, the ghosts net a Pac-topus and drop it in the pool, but the Pac-topus goes after the ghosts instead of Pac-Man. In the meantime, Pac-Baby, Chomp-Chomp and Sour Puss finally escape and start creating havoc aboard the ship. Pac-Baby goes in search of Pac-Man. Chomp-Chomp and Sour Puss get into the ship's control room and spin the large steering wheel. Pac-Man arrives and the ship's captain shouts mutiny if he doesn't take his pets and Pac-Baby away. Later, all is forgiven and Pepper and Pac-Man sit at the captain's table drinking a toast to their anniversary. The ghosts still haven't given up and disguise themselves as a layer cake. Pac-Man gives Pepper the cake, but the ghosts reveal themselves. Pac-Man and Pepper run away and are chased all over the ship. Pac-Man comes across a life-saver ring and inside are power pellets. Pac-Man and Pepper eat them and chomp the ghosts. Pac-Baby also gets into the chomping fun and the family is reunited. In the end, Chomp-Chomp and Sour Puss knock Pac-Man overboard where he is happier to be away from all the chaos onboard.

Pac-Mania bumper: The ghosts ride atop each other on a unicycle chasing Pac-Man. The bottom ghosts sneezes, disrupting their chase and Pac-Man says that he's nothing to sneeze at.

22. The Great Power-Pellet Robbery (December 4, 1982) Story uncredited

There's a speeding fire engine driven by the ghosts in disguise. They ask a Pac-policeman about a fictitious fire in the power forest and the policeman gives them a police escort directly there. He actually escorts the ghosts to a dead end with Pac-Man who says that power pellet trees are fireproof. Pac-Man and a number of other Pac-people eat some power pellets and chomp the ghosts. The chomped ghosts go back to Mezmaron to get new clothes. Mezmaron says that Pac-Man is on a special mission transporting a large amount of power pellets in an armored car. He sends the ghosts in a special high-speed super car to chase after Pac-Man, but Pac-Man defeats their plans at every turn. The supercar is also a super copter and they continue to chase Pac-Man in his truck and lift the truck up off the ground by a giant magnet. Pac-Man radios for help. A man in a Pac-plane helps and he detaches Pac-Man and the truck and sends Pac-missiles that chomp the ghost copters propellers. The ghosts land in a henhouse and are nibbled on by tiny chicks. Meanwhile, Pac-Man's mission is almost complete, but the ghosts come back in their supercar again. Pac-Man is low on fuel and fills the truck and himself with some power pellets. Now, Pac-Man and the truck chase and chomp the ghosts. The remaining ghosts go into the Pac-cafe and hide in a jukebox. Pac-Man plays a tune which chomps the remaining ghosts. The chomped ghosts escape and manage to take the armored truck to Mezmaron. Mezmaron opens the truck, but it's filled with fireworks, not power pellets. Soon, the fireworks go off, annoying Mezmaron and the ghosts. Pac-Man wonders why they wanted the fireworks anyway.

23. A Bad Case of the Chomps (December 11, 1982) Story uncredited

Pac-Man is shaving in the morning, but the faucet is busted in the sink. He asks Chomp-Chomp to fetch his tool box to fix it, but can't. The bathroom floods and when Pepper opens the door, water and Pac-Man washes out. Pac-Man calls

Pete the plumber for help. The ghosts attack the plumber before he gets to Pac-Man and take his truck. At Pac-Man's house, Pac-Man asks where Pete is and soon the ghosts start chasing Pac-Man. Pepper walks in with power pellets and she and Pac-Man eat and chomp the ghosts. Amazingly, Pac-Man fixes the sink while chomping the ghosts. Now, Pac-Man has a toothache, so Pepper takes him to the dentist. The ghosts go back to Mezmaron's place for new suits. Pac-Man has a bad case of the chomps and chompitis and has to be in the hospital for a few days. The ghosts take over Dr. Hackensaw's office and pretend to be the therapist for Pac-Man. Pac-Man smells a rat, but before he can do anything a nurse takes Pac-Man for his physical. The ghosts disguise themselves as the doctors for the physical and somehow end up getting chomped by Pac-Man. Clyde manages to tie up Pac-Man, but even he fails and gets chomped. The real doctor comes in and says he actually suffers from ghostitis, which is good. Pac-Man gets released from the hospital, but then feels ill again when he gets the bill.

Pac-Mania bumper: Mezmaron tells the ghosts to get Pac-Man without bungling, but once again they are caught in their own trap.

24. Goo-Goo at the Zoo (December 11, 1982) Story uncredited

Pac-Man lays out some power pellets for Chomp-Chomp to eat in order to get him to take a bath. Pac-Man ends up in the tub. Pepper comes into the garage and reminds him that he was going to take Pac-Baby to the zoo. The Pac family goes to the zoo. Pepper is a bit nervous, but Pac-Man is not as the animals are in cages. The animals still manage to kiss Pac-Man with big sloppy kisses. Pac-Baby wants to play with a Pac-gorilla baby, but the gorilla's mother doesn't want him to. The Pacs take a family photo and discuss what to do next.

While discussing, Pac-Baby releases the gorilla baby. Soon, Pac-Baby is releasing all the animals as he gets the zookeeper's keys. Pac-Man tries to round up all of the released animals, but they all escape from the zoo causing traffic accidents in town. The animals head to the pastry shop and they all start eating pastries. Pac-Man is stuck with a $400 bill for the pastries the animals ate. Now the animals run into a department store and harass the customers. Pac-Man is still trying to round them up. Pepper shows up and says that Pac-Man has to save Pac-Baby over all the animals. The gorilla is climbing a building with Pac-Man in a way that echoes King Kong while Pac-Man tries to rescue her with a plane and power pellets. He then climbs the wall after the gorilla. Finally, the gorilla is on top of the building with Pac-Baby and a number of other animals that are some power pellets, so they seem dangerous, but Pac-Baby directs them back down off the building and to Pac-Man's home. In the end, Pac-Man and Pepper play host to all the animals in their home, which becomes the new home for the zoo.

25. The Pac-Mummy (December 18, 1982) Story uncredited
Note: For some reason, the picture quality of this episode and #26 are inferior on the DVD set, but not the bumper.

The ghosts have a transmitter that will transmit them through the telephone lines. They try to get sent to the power forest, but instead are sent to the football stadium where Pac-Man is playing. The ghosts end up in the middle of a football game and get chomped. They go back to Mezmaron's to get new suits. Mezmaron sends the ghosts to the museum to get a mummy to help him carry out his plans. Pepper and Pac-Baby are at the museum and they call Pac-Man because the mummy is on the loose. The ghosts disguise themselves as mummies as they don't want the mummy to get all the credit for Mezmaron's plans. Pac-Man sees through their disguise and asks where Pepper is or he'll chomp them. The ghosts say that Pepper and Pac-Baby are with Mezmaron and the mummy in the Pac-pyramid. Pac-Man arrives at the pyramid and Mezmaron instructs the mummy to chomp him. The ghosts are now there, too, and try to chomp, but Pac-Baby finds some power pellets in the pyramid. The mummy eats power pellets too and he turns on Mezmaron and chases him and also chomps ghosts.

Pac-Mania bumper: Chomp-Chomp is sleeping. Sour Puss throws pies on him from a hot air balloon, but as usual everything backfires and Sour Puss pops the balloon and gets hit with her own pies.

26. Nighty Nightmares (December 18, 1982) Story uncredited
Pac-Man is making a ship in a bottle. Chomp-Chomp sleeps while Sour Puss puts fleas on him. The fleas bite Chomp-Chomp and wake him up and he starts scratching. Sour Puss laughs hysterically and soon the chasing animals disrupt the ship in the bottle. Pepper reminds Pac-Man to go to bed. Mezmaron is also sleeping in his lair and the ghosts come in to get a gizmo without disturbing him. The gizmo makes people have nightmares, but it backfires and makes the ghosts sleep. The ghosts have a nightmare where they are in a court accused of chomping. The court finds the ghosts guilty and the ghosts are sentenced to a

Pac-attack and chomped. Another nightmare shows the ghosts in a boxing ring fighting Pac-Man. Pac-Man eats power pellets and chomps the ghosts. A third nightmare shows Sue running away from a giant snail. She meets up with Pepper who says that the only way out of the dream is to get chomped. Soon, Sue is caught in a spider web and gets chomped by Pepper. A fourth nightmare shows a Pac-funhouse where a ghost chases Pac-Man. Pac-Man runs into the hall of mirrors which confuses the ghost and he gets chomped. A fifth nightmare shows the ghosts and Pac-Man on a gigantic chess board. Pac-Man is the king and Pepper the queen. The various chess pieces chase and chomp the ghosts. In the end, Pac-Man wakes up and explains the wacky dream he had about the ghosts having a nightmare machine.

Also:

*Pac-Man Halloween Special* (October 30, 1982) Story by Jeffrey Scott

Repeat segments of "Pacula" and "Trick or Chomp". See episode descriptions above.

*Christmas Comes to Pac-Land* (December 16, 1982) Story by Jeffrey Scott

Pac-Land is covered in snow and Santa Claus flies by with all of the reindeer including Rudolph. Santa checks his list. The Pacs build a snowman and then go on a toboggan ride, pets included. Meanwhile, the ghosts sing "Jingle Bells" and come across the family tobogganing. The ghosts set out to chomp them. Chomp-Chomp barks and Sour Puss hisses at them as the ghosts chase them all. The Pacs crash and start looking for power pellets, but the ghosts have taken them all, so the Pac family starts hurling snowballs at the ghosts. Inky accidentally throws some of them power pellets and the family eats them and start chomping the ghosts. Santa Claus is falling behind schedule and gets hit by the ghost eyes, knocking Santa and his sleigh out of the sky. The Pacs and others come across the crashed sleigh and reindeers and Santa. Santa tries to get back into the sky, but the reindeer and the sleigh are in too bad of shape, so the Pacs take them in to warm them up with some cocoa by the fire. Pac-Man and Pepper ask who he is and what he does and what Christmas is. Santa is incredulous that they don't know, but he explains everything. The Pac people agree to help Santa and his reindeer back in the air before midnight. Finally, the ghost eyes return to Mezmaron's hideout and get back into some new clothes. They plan their revenge on the Pacs. Meanwhile, Pac-Man and Chomp-Chomp search for Santa's missing bag of toys lost outside in the snow. The ghosts come back to Pac-Land and discover Santa's sack filled with toys and start playing with them. Pac-Man discovers that the ghosts have found Santa's toys. They decide to burrow under the snow and grab the sack. Unfortunately, Pac-Man and Chomp-Chomp are caught by the ghosts and are soon going to be chomped. Pac-Man says he only wants the toys and starts running. He tells Chomp-Chomp to save the toys while ghosts are chasing him. Pinky and Blinky split off to get Chomp-Chomp, but he hides. Pac-Man is not so lucky and he gets chomped. After the ghosts leave, Chomp-Chomp drags Santa's bag to Pac-Man and with his remaining strength, they go back home. Santa tells Pac-Baby "Twas the Night Before Christmas", while his reindeer are improving. Pac-Man is passing out, but he keeps trying to go on. Before they make it home, they fall off a cliff and the toys scatter. Pac-Man and Chomp-Chomp slowly repack Santa's bag. Pepper is concerned about where Pac-Man is. He finally shows up totally frozen and Chomp-Chomp drags in Santa's sack. Pepper gives Pac-Man some cocoa which gives back some of his strength. Santa says that, unfortunately, it is now too late and that he has missed Christmas. Santa says that even if his reindeer were jet-propelled, he couldn't save Christmas. That gives Pac-Man an idea and they go to help them out, but are soon stopped by ghosts again. Pac-Man pleads with the ghosts and tells them the story of Christmas. The ghosts have a heart and let Pac-Man and Santa go, and they all go straight to the power pellet forest. Pac-Man tells the reindeer to chomp power pellets and they get their strength back. They see Santa off and he makes his deliveries just in time for Christmas. The Pacs go home to discover a Christmas tree and many presents. Everyone is happy as they have saved Christmas. The ghosts decide to rescind their decision to not chomp, but Pac-Man gives them presents, so they decide not to chomp again.

### Season two (1983-1984) as part of *The Pac-Man/Rubik, the Amazing Cube Hour*:

The opening on all season two episodes show Pac-Man fleeing the ghosts (Inky, Blinky, Pinky, Clyde and Sue), but this time a hole opens up in the sky to reveal Super-Pac, who swoops down to rescue Pac-Man, who promptly crashes into a tree. Pac-Man is dropped from the tree into the sidecar of a motorcycle driven by P.J. The standard Pac-Man theme song plays in the background and a deep-voiced person announces "Pac-Man". Next, Pepper and Pac-Baby drive by to feed Pac-Man power pellets which give him, Pepper and Pac-Baby the strength to chomp ghosts. As the ghost eyes float away, Mezmaron is shown watching this on his viewscreen in disgust and he slaps his forehead. The title "Pac-Man" is revealed with the standard Hanna-Barbera orchestral crash.

27. Here's Super-Pac (September 17, 1983) Story uncredited

The ghosts plan yet another attack on Pac-Land by driving a red tank. Pac-Man and Pepper are out for a relaxing drive and get stuck behind the tank. The ghosts shoot "guk" out of the tank's cannon which splatters everywhere and traps Pac-Man's car in its tracks. The ghosts demand to know where the power pellet forest is. Suddenly, Super-Pac drops out of a hole in the sky. Super-Pac is somewhat dimwitted. He tries to stop the ghosts who shoot out some guk on him. The ghosts try to run Super-Pac over, but destroy their tank in the process. Super-Pac traps two of the ghosts with the old "one-two" which is literally a one and a two number shape. Pepper is impressed with Super-Pac and brings him home to Pac-Man's house. Super-Pac plays with Chomp-Chomp by flinging a fetch bone a far distance, and then flips Pac-Baby in the air way up high through the roof. Soon, they all sit down to eat and Super-Pac sucks up the soup and half of Pac-Man's house with his super breath. Meanwhile, Mezmaron is informed of Super-Pac by the ghosts and he sends a super chomping robot. Super-Pac repairs Pac-Man's house and then flies away. Pepper goes to retrieve Super-Pac to defeat the robot who is now chomping Pac-Land buildings. Mezmaron announces that he will chomp all of Pac-Land unless the power pellet forest is turned over to him. Super-Pac eats a super power pellet and goes to chomp the robot and then starts chomping everything in sight. Pac-Man finds Super-Pac's time hole to get rid of him.

Pac-Mania bumper: A ship's captain asks Super-Pac for help, but ends up sticking the ship into a gigantic bottle.

28. Hey, Hey, Hey, It's P.J. (September 17, 1983) Story uncredited

Pac-Man tries to get a Pac-fly while he and Chomp-Chomp clean up. Sour Puss tries to sabotage everything with a bicycle pump which backfires. Finally the room is clean as Pac-Man's cousin P.J. shows up, who is similar in behavior to *Happy Days*' Fonz character. P.J. has dropped out of school and says he is now going to live in Pac-Man's garage. P.J. then proceeds to clean out the refrigerator, steaming Pac-Man. P.J. then takes Pac-Baby for a ride on his motorcycle. Pac-Man chases them at full-speed to stop them, but then can't stop and causes a car accident. Pepper tells Pac-Man that he has to convince P.J. to go back to school. P.J. is playing pool and Pac-Man tells him to try Pac-Land school. If he likes it, he has to go back to school. While on their way, P.J. reveals that he's going to have a garage party that night. Pac-Man takes P.J. to Pac-physics class. P.J. heckles the teacher, but Pac-Man gets in trouble and has to demonstrate the law of gravity in front of the class. Next, Pac-Man takes P.J. to drama class which is currently performing Shakespeare. P.J. is not impressed, and feels he can do a better job of acting. Next, is Pac-gym. Pac-Man says that if he likes gym, he could be an expert in sports. Pac-Man is recruited to work out on the rings. Pac-Man treats P.J. to lunch in the cafeteria, so P.J. overloads his tray. A bully picks on Pac-Man in the cafeteria and Pac-Man gets the blame when the principal shows up. Pac-Man gets kicked out of school, but P.J. is convinced to go back to school; however, he is going to keep going to Pac-Land school instead of his old school and continue to live in Pac-Man's garage, where his party is about to begin with dozens of girls.

29. The Super-Pac-Bowl (September 24, 1983) Story uncredited

It's the Super-Pac-Bowl and Pepper and Pac-Baby are cheering from the stands. Pac-Man is on the Power-Pellet Pickers playing against the Packensack Packers. A coin is tossed just as the ghosts appear out of a hole in the middle of the game. Pac-Man runs and then says he gives up, but the ghosts would rather chomp all of the other players on the team. The ghosts take the team's place and

play against Pac-Man's team. Everytime one of Pac-Man's team gets the ball, the ghosts chomp him, but are called foul for chomping. Quarterback Pac-Man tries to throw the ball, but it sticks to his hand. The ghosts get a touchdown, but it is taken back for a tarball. Pac-Man is ready to give up when Super-Pac drops out of a hole in the sky. Pac-Man asks Super-Pac if he can play football. Mezmaron helps the ghosts with a guided propeller ball. Super-Pac catches it, but it flies him around. He lands outside the stadium and attracts Chomp-Chomp, who bites his suit. Super-Pac comes back to the stadium and eventually the ball lands on the five-yard line for the ghost advantage. The ghosts finally score a legitimate touchdown and the score is now 86-0. Pac-Man says Super-Pac has to chomp on one of his superpower pellets. The ghosts steal it before he can eat it, but Super-Pac manages to get it back, chomps the ghosts and scores multiple touchdowns, enough to win the game. Super-Pac can't stop and he chomps the gridiron and chases Mezmaron away who says he will release the captured football team. Now Pac-Man and Pepper have to stop Super-Pac before he chomps the whole town, and they do.

Pac-Mania bumper: Pac-Man and P.J. goes Pac-surfing. Pac-Man is not very good and smashes through some changing rooms and dunes.

30. Journey Into the Pac-Past (September 24, 1983) Story uncredited

Pac-Man is looking for his socks and Chomp-Chomp licks his feet. He finds his socks in the washer, but it has eaten his socks. To save on repair bills,

Pac-Man tries to repair the washer. Soon, P.J. shows up and starts repairing the machine. P.J. repairs it so that now it is a time machine and he and Pac-Man travel back to ancient Egypt. He says it's 2500 B.C, before chomping. Some Egyptians show up and call him Tutanpac-man and want to bury him. P.J. has a plan to rescue him and he grabs Pac-Man while aboard a chariot. They speed back to the time machine and they go to a different era just in time. Now they are on a pirate ship with Pac-beard the pirate. Pac-beard makes Pac-Man and P.J. walk the plank, but P.J. mentions a treasure in order to save them. Pac-Man says this fictional treasure is buried on a nearby island, which turns out to be a whale. The whale shoots water out of its spout because he's angry that everyone is messing with him and soon Pac-Man and P.J. are traveling through time again. Now they are with Wilbur and Orville Pac who are trying to invent a lawnmower that just so happens to look like an airplane. P.J. helps the Pacs to fly The Spirit of P.J. plane. They are successful until the plane starts to nosedive. P.J. and Pac-Man time travel again, while Wilbur and Orville decide to invent the video game. P.J. and Pac-Man arrive home. P.J. notices his sweater is dirty so he sticks it in the washer and they time travel again. Pepper says to Pac-Baby to remind her to have P.J. fix the TV when they get back.

31. Public Pac-Enemy No. 1 (October 1, 1983) Story uncredited

Out at sea, police are patrolling the Pac-Land jail on Pacatraz. The Pac-prisoner escapes and rows a boat to the mainland. In the meantime, Pac-Man is watching an old Pac Bogart movie. A news report breaks about the prisoner on the loose, but Pac-Man doesn't hear as he heads to the kitchen to get some Pac-cookies with Chomp-Chomp. Next morning, Chomp-Chomp goes to retrieve the paper and sees the crook. He tries to alert Pac-Man who thinks Chomp-Chomp is just behaving strangely. Pac-Man goes to work and on the way goes to the bank. The bank teller gives Pac-Man bags of money as she thinks he's Pretty Boy Pac. Secretly, she has called the police who have arrived to arrest Pac-Man. Meanwhile, the real Pretty Boy discovers he looks like Pac-Man and goes home to his house. Pepper sees Pretty Boy as Pac-Man and is wondering why he's at home instead of at work. Pretty Boy lies and says he has a holiday and is rehearsing for a play about prisoners. The real Pac-Man is getting his mug shot taken and keeps saying he's not Pretty Boy. Pretty Boy starts putting on Pac-Man's clothes, but Chomp-Chomp is not fooled and growls at Pretty Boy. Pretty Boy locks himself in the bathroom, but his ball and chain keeps slowing him down and Chomp-Chomp still chases him. Pac-Man gets a phone call and calls home. The phone is answered by Pretty Boy who pretends to be Pac-Man. The call is useless and Pac-Man is sent back to his cell. In the cell, another prisoner named Tiny threatens Pac-Man who thinks he's Pretty Boy. Tiny wants Pretty Boy to help him escape, so Pac-Man does. The escape makes the news and the real Pretty Boy sees it on Pac-Man's TV. Pretty Boy decides to lay low in Pac-Man's house. Meanwhile, Pac-Man and Tiny get involved in a high speed car chase avoiding the police, but eventually they get caught. Pretty Boy is trapped inside Pac-Man's house with Chomp-Chomp and Sour Puss chomping on him.

Pretty Boy has had enough and decides he'd rather be in the slammer. He goes back to Pacatraz and the real Pac-Man is released. Pepper finally reads the paper just as the freshly released Pac-Man comes home still with HIS ball and chain. Pepper is scared and sics Chomp-Chomp and Sour Puss on him and as the scene fades Pac-Man is being chased by his own pets up the street.

Pac-Mania bumper: The wrecking ball is out of control and Super-Pac comes to the rescue. He destroys the wrecking ball, but has to become one so that the driver can finish his job.

32. The Old Pac-Man and the Sea (October 1, 1983) Story uncredited

A garbage scow with Pac-Man aboard sails by a small island. Pac-Man is concerned about the Pacuda Triangle. He reveals to the barge captain that the garbage is disguising the biggest power pellet shipment. Meanwhile, Mezmaron and the ghosts are in their submarine and discover the garbage scow. Mezmaron commands the ghosts to shoot a torpedo. There are no torpedoes as the ghosts are the torpedo and Mezmaron fires the ghosts toward the barge who begin to chomp at the barge and sink it. Now, they have to get the barge to Mezmaron but it sinks so far as they all discover the sunken city of Paclantis. The Pactantis people take Pac-Man, the captain and the ghosts to their queen. Pac-Man and the captain are selected to do a chomp chase while the ghosts are sent to prison. The ghosts escape as do Pac-Man and the captain, but it was all a trick to get them all into the coliseum to do the chomp chase as gladiators. Pac-Man and the captain are at a disadvantage as they have no power pellets and they are chomped by the ghosts. Mezmaron is wondering where the ghosts and the barge went and he discovers Paclantis. Mezmaron tries to take the supply of power pellets. In doing so, many of them spill out down where Pac-Man and the captain are and they eat a bunch and start chomping ghosts. For saving Paclantis, the queen offers her ugly daughter's hand in marriage. Pac-Man says he's already married, which doesn't seem to dissuade anyone and in the end Pac-Man is chased by the daughter.

33. The Greatest Show in Pacland (October 8, 1983) Story uncredited

In a small shack at the base of Mezmaron's lair, the ghosts celebrate Dinky's birthday. Meanwhile, Pac-Baby is searching for Pac-Man and Pepper at home. It turns out to be a surprise party for Pac-Baby. Pac-Man says they are going to go to the circus for Pac-Baby's birthday. Dinky is causing trouble at his party, so the ghosts give in and take him to the circus, too. A vendor is selling ghost balloons and Pac-Baby chomps them forcing Pac-Man to purchase them all. Dinky is still complaining even at the circus. They try to go in, but ghosts are forbidden to go into the circus. The ghosts disguise themselves as clowns in order to sneak in. Soon, they encounter the Pac family and fool them, but soon they take off their clown suits and try to chomp the Pacs. Pepper hides in a barrel and Pac-Man hides in a cannon and is immediately shot out of it. Dinky and Pac-Baby still like each other and pal around. Pac-Man then sees Dinky and Pac-Baby on top of the high wire and both the ghosts and Pac-Man try to save them, even though they are not in any danger. The ghosts and Pac-Man eventually fall, but are caught by trapezes. They all fall again, but are caught by a net, and the ghosts try to chomp Pac-Man again. Now, Dinky and Pac-Baby are in the lion's cage and the ghosts and Pac-Man try to save them here, too. As usual, they are not in any real danger. Soon, Pac-Man is lion taming with a whip and a chair. Pepper doesn't seem to do anything except appear distraught, but finally Dinky and Pac-Baby are caught in a cage so they can be watched. For their next birthday, they plan to go to the wild animal park.

Pac-Mania bumper: Super-Pac does skywriting to earn extra money. He is soon chased by ghosts, but Super-Pac creates a cloud Pac-Man to chomp them.

34. Pac-a-Thon (October 8, 1983) Story uncredited

Pac-Man is lighting the torch at the latest Pac-a-Thon. The first event will be the shotput. Then, the hammer throw. Chomp-Chomp and Sour Puss cause mischief during these events by retrieving the shotput and interrupting the hammer throw. Next, is weightlifting and Pac-Man participates. He lifts it, but the weights have fallen off. The ghosts show up and want to participate in events and they start winning them. Next, is the high dive competition. The diver balks as there is a shark in the pool. Pac-Man dives and does a huge belly-flop. Interestingly, he dives without his hat, but keeps his shoes. The ghosts dive, too, and win with a swan dive. Even still, Pac-Man is in the lead with the ghosts in second place. Next, is canoeing. The ghosts cheat by pulling the giant plug at the

bottom of the river, preventing the Pacs from winning as they can't move in the mud, while the ghosts float over the finish line in their balloon canoe. The final event is the De-Pac-a-lon with five grueling events. The ghosts are now ahead so Pac-Man must win. The ghosts chomp Punjab the pole vaulter and he is out of the competition. Pac-Man is next, but also fails. Pac-Man's only hope is to win the 1000 maze run and the ghosts are ahead 1000 points to 1. The ghosts are chasing Pac-Man more than trying to win, but Pac-Man doesn't know this and needs some energy. Pepper, on the sidelines, gives Pac-Man some power pellets and he starts chomping ghosts with Chomp-Chomp, Sour Puss, Pepper, and Pac-Baby also participating in the fun and in the end they all win gold medals and the Pac-a-Thon.

35. The Genii of Pacdad (October 15, 1983) Story uncredited

The Pac family is at the beach. Pepper is sunbathing. Pac-Man was fishing and is now helping Pac-Baby to build a sand castle only to be interrupted by Chomp-Chomp, who builds a better one. Pac-Man goes back to his fishing and starts reeling in a big one... a bottle! He rubs it and a Genii appears but Pac-Man doesn't see him so he tosses the bottle away. Of course the ghosts are also at the beach. One of them needs suntan lotion, sees the bottle and starts pouring which in turn rubs the bottle and releases the Genii again. The ghosts are scared until the Genii says whoever holds the bottle controls him and gets three wishes. The ghosts fight for the bottle and start asking for wishes. They waste their wishes on wishing the others would shut up and then wishing to reverse it. They only have one wish left so they wish for one million more wishes which is granted. Pac-Man is still failing at fishing and now he's being troubled by the ghosts with the Genii. The ghosts say that power pellets will not help him as long as they have their wishes. Suddenly, Super-Pac shows up, but he's not much help as the Genii tosses him away and Super-Pac inadvertently takes Pac-Man with him through the space hole back to Super-Pac's home which looks like the Sea of Holes from *Yellow Submarine*. Now, the duo are on the search for the correct hole to get back to the beach, and there are four billion holes. Eventually, they do find the correct one and get back to the beach. Pac-Man also gets control of the bottle and does a wish. Then the ghosts grab the bottle and wish. Then Super-Pac grabs the bottle and wishes. All of the wishes and results are really stupid and useless until Super-Pac wishes for superpower power pellets. Super-Pac starts chomping ghosts before anyone else can grab the bottle and make a wish. He takes care of the ghosts, but also starts damaging everything else. Pac-Man finally gets the bottle and wishes that Super-Pac would go back into his time hole before he does any more damage. Relieved of Super-Pac, Pac-Baby gets the bottle and wishes for a bunch of Super-Pacs, which in the end are all flying around the sky as Pac-Man does a deep sigh.

Pac-Mania bumper: Pac-Man is mowing the lawn, when P.J. shows up to supe up his mower. Now, the mower is super-charged and Pac-Man cuts down trees and creates a giant "HELP!" with the bushes.

36. P.J. Goes Pac-Hollywood (October 15, 1983) Story uncredited.

The Pacs are traveling to Pac-Hollywood for the first time and are excited to possibly meet some big stars. They go to 20th Century Pac Studios to see P.J., who is going to be in a film called *Ghost Encounters*. They find P.J. among some adoring fans. P.J. is informed that his stand-in is sick and filming must stop. Pepper suggests that Pac-Man fill-in for the stand-in and filming continues. Pac-Man heads to make-up to look more like P.J. Of course, as a stand-in, Pac-Man gets beat up and injured, while P.J. is given the star treatment and not in danger at all. In one scene, Pac-Man suffers all the disasters that befell Indiana Jones in his first film with falling rocks and snakes and spider webs. After shooting the scene, Pepper asks Pac-Man if he's all right. He says he's fine and passes out. The ghosts were bound to show up at sometime and here they are. They are at the studios to take a studio tour. The studio guard thinks they are actors and he sends them to the same stage as the P.J. film. Soon, the costumed ghosts who are supposed to be in the film show up, but the studio guard sends them away. So, the real ghosts are in the film and ready to start chomping. In the next scene, Pac-Man rescues the girl from lava. She opens a door and escapes. Pac-Man opens a different door and finds the ghosts. Pac-Man starts running and the director starts screaming that they aren't real, just actors. Pac-Man disagrees. Fortunately, P.J. eats some power pellets and chomps the ghosts. It is all caught on film and in the end they screen the film and it looks like it will be a hit. The director is so happy he offers Pac-Man another film called *How the West was Chomped*.

37. Dr. Jekyll and Mr. Pac-Man (October 22, 1983) Story uncredited

In Mezmaron's lair, he is conducting a medical operation with the ghosts assisting. Finally, after 10 years of research, Mezmaron reveals that he has created synthetic power pellets and now he is able to clone his own. In order to see if they work, he wants Pac-Man to eat them. To further entice him, Mezmaron puts chocolate syrup on them. Meanwhile, Pac-Man is practicing his golfing at home. The ghosts disguise themselves as scouts and sell Pepper the synthetic power pellets. Pac-Man readily eats them and then immediately feels sick until he hiccups. The ghosts are disappointed and go home to tell Mezmaron. That night, Pac-Man transforms into a hideous monster and starts stalking the neighborhood. Pac-Man transforms back and finds himself in his neighbor Morris's bedroom. The full moon comes out again and Pac-Man becomes the monster again. Morris hides in his piano, but the monster finds him. Morris calls the police just as Pac-Man reverts back to himself. Pac-Man decides to go home and is warned by police that a werewolf is in the neighborhood. As the police officer is describing the monster, Pac-Man turns into the monster. Meanwhile, the ghosts arrive back at Mezmaron's place and tell him the bad news. Soon, Pac-Man as the monster arrives to eat the ghosts, but before he can chomp, Pac-Man turns back into himself. Mezmaron figures out how Pac-Man transforms by the moonlight and repeatedly draws and then reopens the drapes. He remains Pac-Man and the ghosts chase him. Pac-Man feeds the ghosts some synthetic power pellets and they start chasing Mezmaron as monsters.

Pac-Mania bumper: Pepper is cleaning the house when the ghosts show up. They start chasing her but Pepper sweeps them up and chomps them with her vacuum cleaner.

38. Around the World in 80 Chomps (October 22, 1983) Story uncredited

At the Pac-Land bowling alley there is a bowling competition underway. Of course, Pac-Man is playing. The ghosts are there disguised as multi-colored balls. They soon reveal themselves and start chasing the various participants. Pac-Man orders some power pellets from a nearby burger stand and starts chomping ghosts back in the bowling alley. He gets a trophy for chomping the ghosts. The ghosts go back to Mezmaron's place to get new clothes. Mezmaron gives the ghosts an ultimatum. They take a hot air balloon back to Pac-Land powered by the ghosts' hot air, in order to find another power pellet forest. They search high and low. Pac-Man chases them in his own hot air balloon to stop them. Soon, the balloons try to chomp each other and Pac-Man's balloon gets chomped. Pac-Man pumps his balloon back up and returns to the chase. Mezmaron and the ghosts find a power pellet forest. The ghosts go to pick power pellets, but Pac-Man says they need a license to pick, stopping them temporarily. The ghosts and Mezmaron keep traveling the world to find more power pellet trees that they can pick. Soon, they are down in the Antarctic and go into an igloo bar, order cocoa, and ask where they might find more power pellet trees. The bartender turns out to be Pac-Man who reveals that the power pellet trees grow underwater and that the Pac-penguins eat them, so they chase after the ghosts and Mezmaron and chomp them. Pac-Man is left to figure out how to get home and floats away in that general direction in his hot-air balloon.

39. Super-Pac vs. Pac-Ape (October 29, 1983) Story uncredited

Pac-Man combs a stubborn hair on his head and suddenly discovers that he's going to be late for work and rushes off. Outside of Hood's department store, an organ grinder and his monkey perform. At a stoplight, the monkey jumps into Pac-Man's car while he's eating a banana. Pac-Man gets to work and the organ grinder wants his monkey back. The monkey runs off with Pac-Man's lunchbox and then starts to chomp dozens of power pellets from the forest where Pac-Man works and the monkey becomes a gigantic ape. The ape is about to eat Pac-Man, his boss and the organ grinder. They all call for help and Super-Pac shows up, much to Pac-Man's annoyance. Super-Pac tries to stop the ape, but the ape is not deterred. Pac-Man blows some sneezing powder into the ape's face and with his sneeze, propels the three away and into a nearby power pellet tree. The ape now goes towards Pac-Land. Super-Pac proves to be generally useless, going so far as to doing a little soft shoe. Pac-Man charters a plane to get the ape. Meanwhile, the ape reaches through a department store window where Pepper is shopping and he grabs her and climbs to the top of the tall building. Pac-Man tries to shoot the ape down with power pellets, but the ape smacks him out of the sky. Pac-Man is nose-diving and Super-Pac actually saves him. Super-Pac then flies up to the top of the building to get the ape to release Pepper, which he does, and then he stuffs the giant ape into a hole and helps make him good. In the final

scene, everyone is fine and the organ grinder gets his monkey back, who is now nice but still giant size.

Pac-Mania bumper: Pac-Man and Pac-Baby are at the beach and Pac-Man shows Pac-Baby how to build the biggest sand castle, but Pac-Baby shows off his much larger sand castle, and Pac-Man faints.

40. Computer Packy (October 29, 1983) Story uncredited

Pac-Man gets a Pac-age. It turns out to be a home computer. He tries to set it up, but is having trouble. P.J. stops by to help and gets it running in no time. Soon, the duo are playing a video game which goes out of control and scares Chomp-Chomp. After switching the computer off, P.J. resets it to perform functions so that Pac-Man and Pepper don't have to do them. Now, Pepper is impressed because it will save them money. P.J. shows that the computer can help feed Pac-Baby. Soon, Sour Puss is up to her typical shenanigans and short circuits the computer, which now behaves erratically. P.J. fixes it again or at least tries to. This time he fails and the computer burns out and sucks Pac-Baby into the computer. Soon, Pac-Man and P.J. are sucked inside as well and are chased by giant microchips and circuit boards. Pac-Man eats some power pellets to give him some extra energy. Meanwhile outside, Pepper tries to type a message to Pac-Man and P.J. They soon respond that everything's ok. Pac-Man tries lifting a knob to get out of the computer but unleashes the Chess program and is chased by the pieces. Soon, they fall into a hole and find Pac-Baby spinning on the disc drive. Pepper tries printing images and saves the day by printing Pac-Baby, P.J. and Pac-Man out of the computer. In the end, Pac-Baby and P.J. are able to jump off of their printed page, but Pac-Man remains stuck, so P.J. uses him as a flag banner on his motorcycle and rides off into the distance.

41. Pac Van Winkle (November 5, 1983) Story uncredited

Pac-Man and Chomp-Chomp go hiking. Meanwhile, a witch is making brew in her home in the forest. Her brew will make anyone who tastes it sleep for 20 years. Pac-Man and Chomp-Chomp are lost and Pac-Man suggests going to the cottage to ask directions. The witch answers the door and offers him a drink to calm his nerves. He drinks it and Pac-Man wants more. The witch kicks Pac-Man out for being greedy. Soon Pac-Man is sleepy and sits down to take a nap. When he wakes up, he has a long gray beard and is 20 years older. Pac-Man slowly but surely makes it home. He knocks on the door of his home, but ghosts live at what used to be Pac-Man's house. Soon, these ghosts and others start chasing him. When he seems trapped, he falls down a trap door and discovers many hidden Pac-people who inform him that Pac-Man disappeared years ago. He meets up with Pepper, who is now older, and Pac-Baby, who is now all grown up into a man. They explain that the ghosts have taken over Pac-Land. Together, the Pacs try to take their land back, but they need power pellets, so they try to sneak into the forest to get some, disguised as ghosts. They eat some power pellets, but nothing happens, as the power pellets are now stale. The Pacs all get chomped. Afterwards, Pac-Man feels that if he finds the witch, he will somehow be able to go back in time and fix everything. The witch has a potion that will send him back. He drinks it and goes back in time and everything is back to normal. Pac-Man and Chomp-Chomp go home.

Pac-Mania bumper: Pac-Man is chased by ghosts at the Pac National Park, but they are stopped by the Old Pac-ful Geyser and Pac-Man chomps them.

42. Happy Pacs-giving (November 5, 1983) Story uncredited

It's Pacs-giving Day and Pepper has a turkey. Relatives start showing up and they sit down to eat, but first the story of Pacs-giving must be read, much to Pac-Man's chagrin, who is starving. The story shows the Pacs as Pilgrims named Pacland sailing on the Mayflower in order to escape ghosts. Of course, Chomp-Chomp and Sour Puss are aboard and get into mischief. Finally, the ship comes to the new world and Miles Pac-Man names the new colony Pac-Land. Ms. Pac-Man is shown planting power pellet trees in the new land with Chomp-Chomp and Sour Puss getting into more trouble with bees, bears and honey. The Pac-pilgrims had little food so they say grace for more food and better times ahead. Miles and Pac-dog search for more wood and discover Native American ghosts who want to chomp them. To get Miles, they make Inky dress up like a Pac-turkey. Miles goes back to the cabin to warn the others. The sun comes out to reveal fresh power pellets on the trees and all of the Pac-people eat and chomp the ghosts. Since the colony has been saved, a Pacs-giving feast was started and even the ghosts are invited. With the story done, Pac-Man starts gobbling food.

# Pac-Man Model Sheets

PAC-MAN and MS. PAC

# 98 ■ The First Animated TV Show Based Upon a Video Game

Pac-Man Model Sheets ■ 99

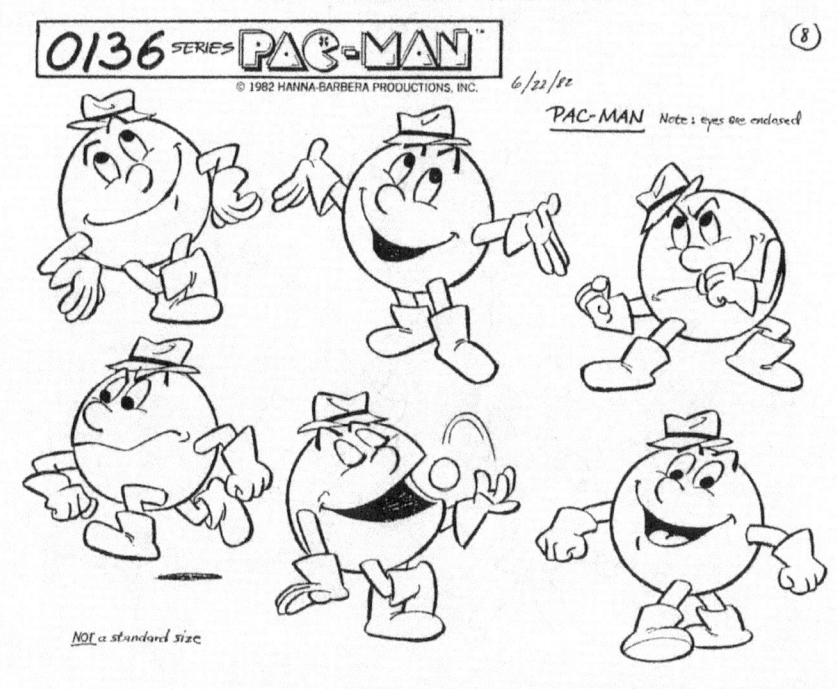

## The First Animated TV Show Based Upon a Video Game

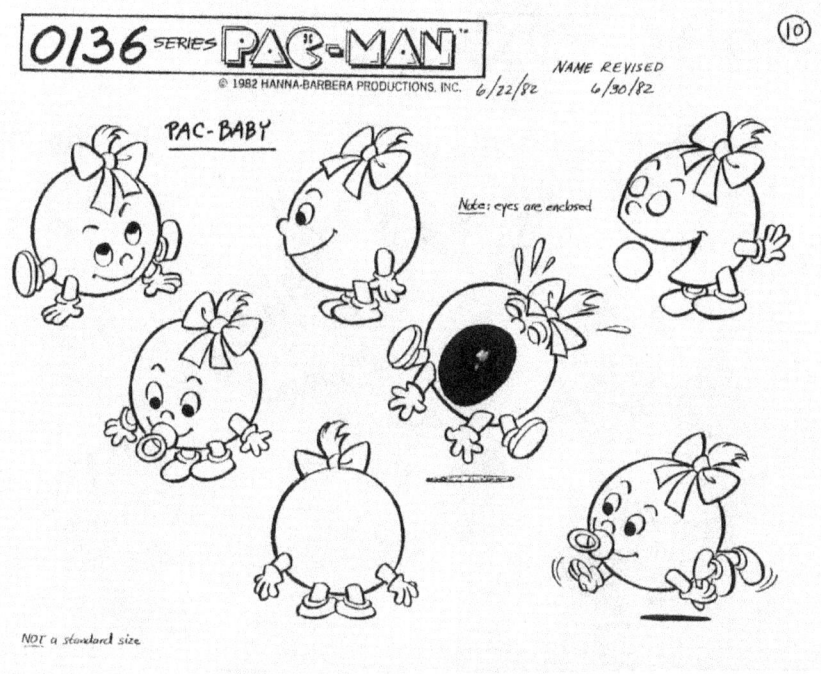

# Pac-Man Model Sheets 103

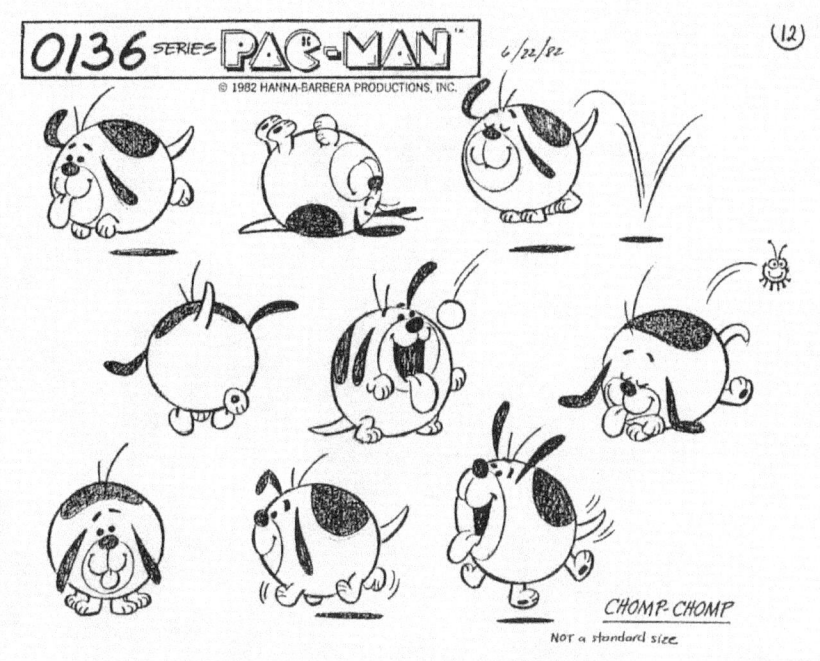

# The First Animated TV Show Based Upon a Video Game

## The First Animated TV Show Based Upon a Video Game

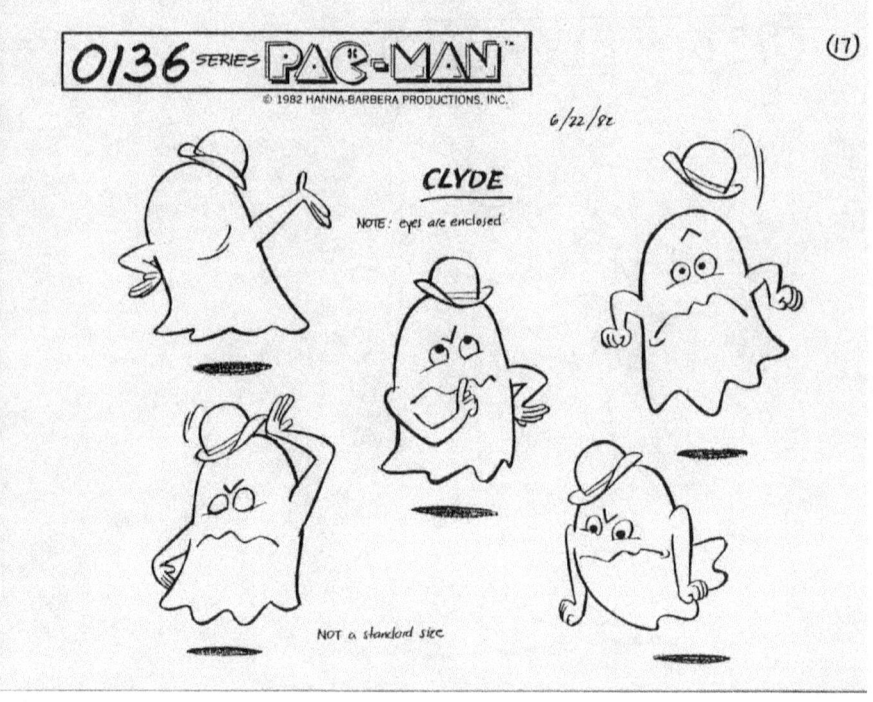

## Pac-Man Model Sheets 107

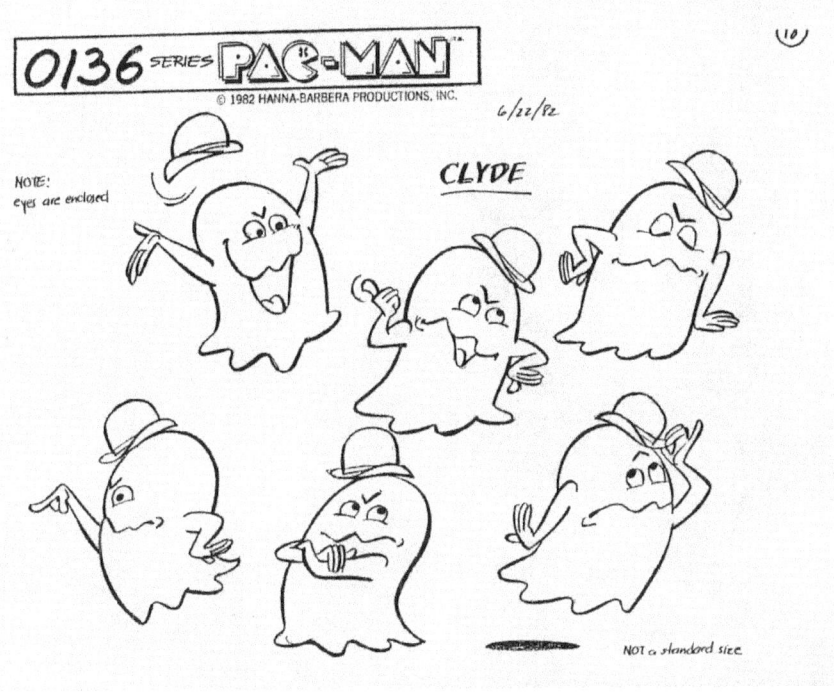

## The First Animated TV Show Based Upon a Video Game

# Pac-Man Model Sheets — 109

## The First Animated TV Show Based Upon a Video Game

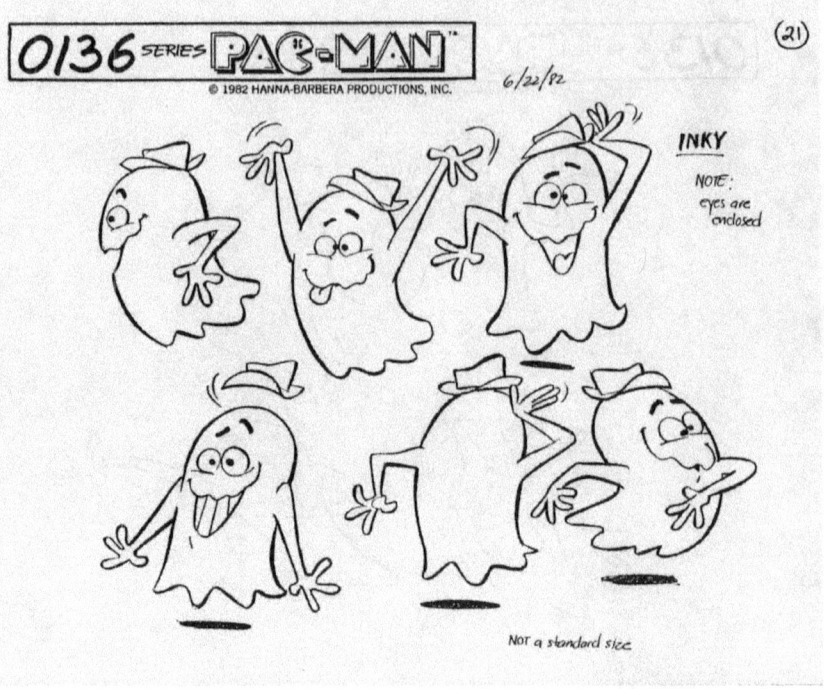

## Pac-Man Model Sheets • 111

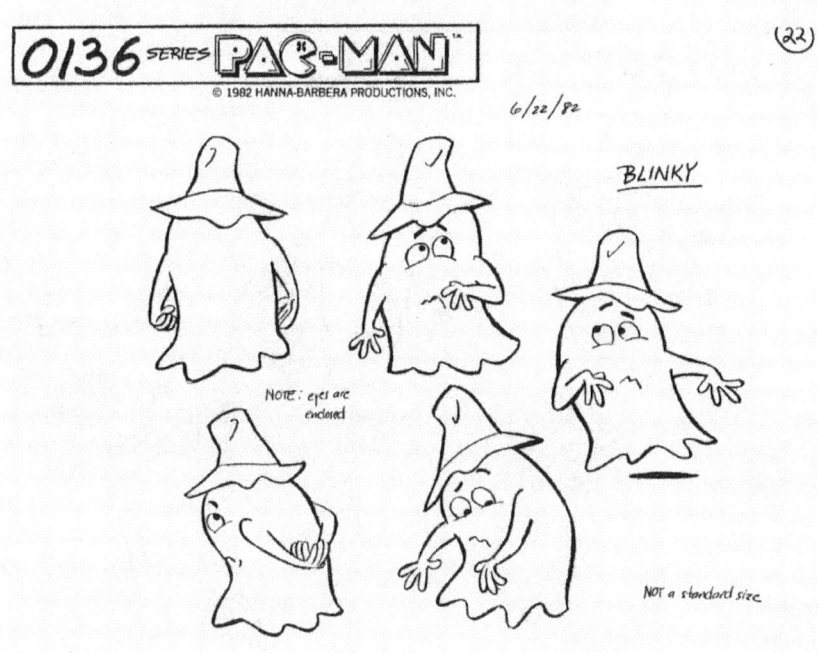

## The First Animated TV Show Based Upon a Video Game

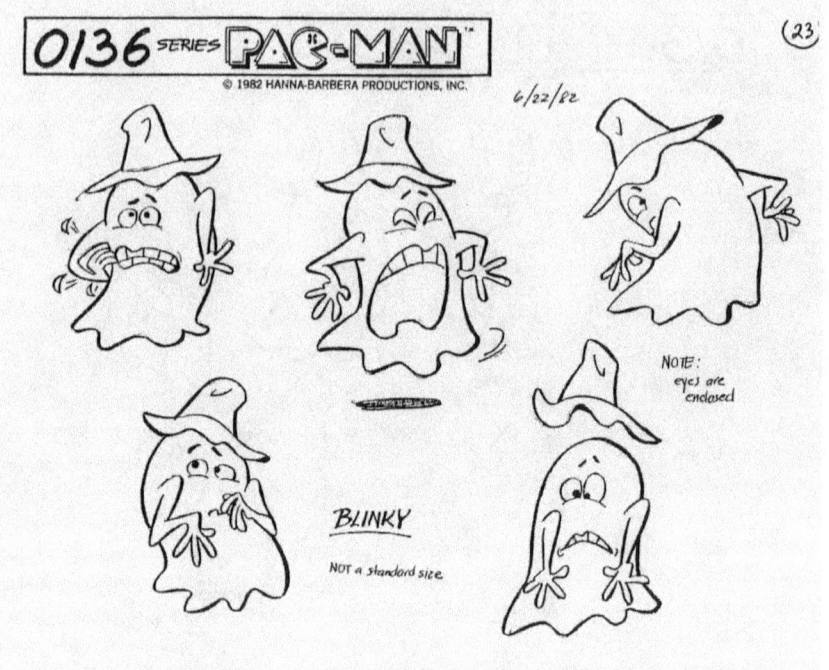

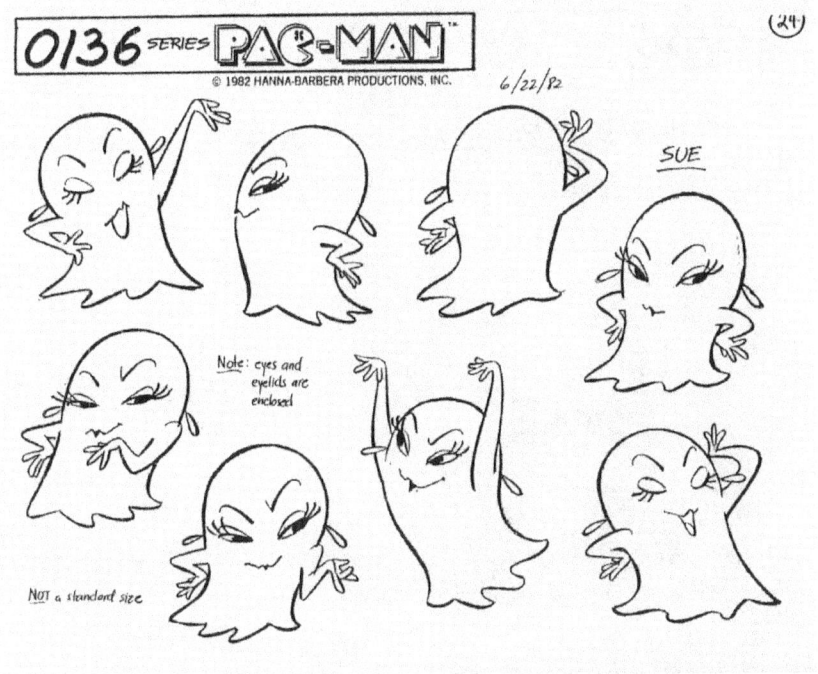

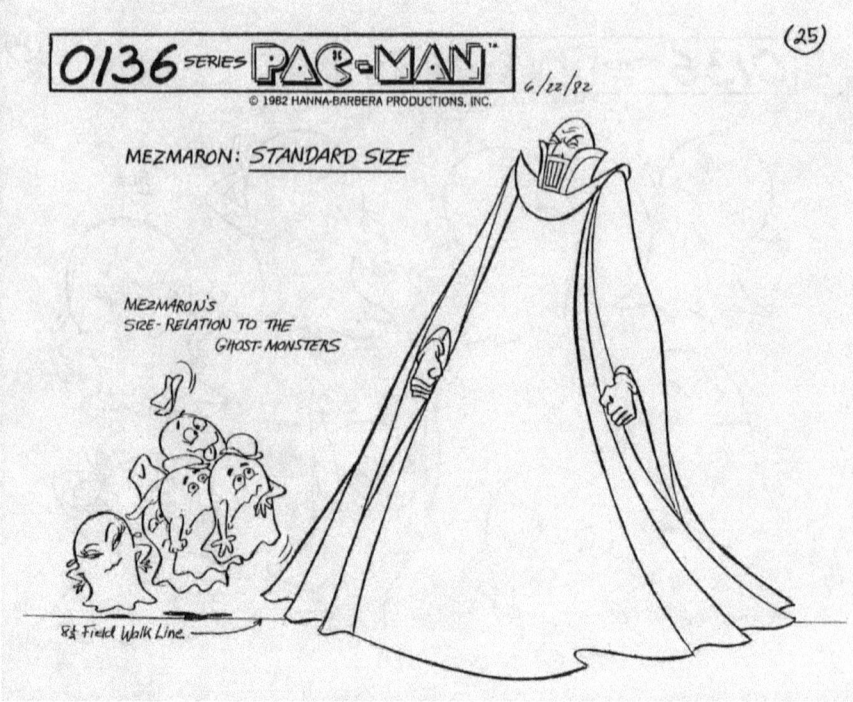

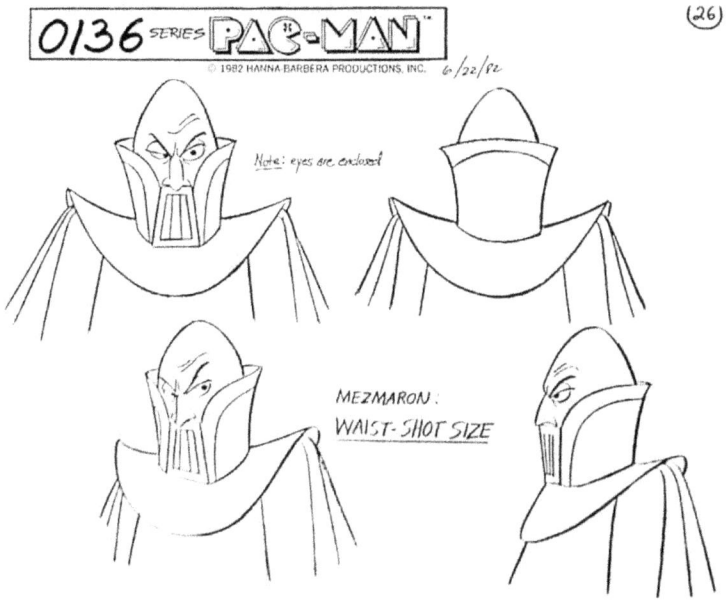

### 116 ■ The First Animated TV Show Based Upon a Video Game

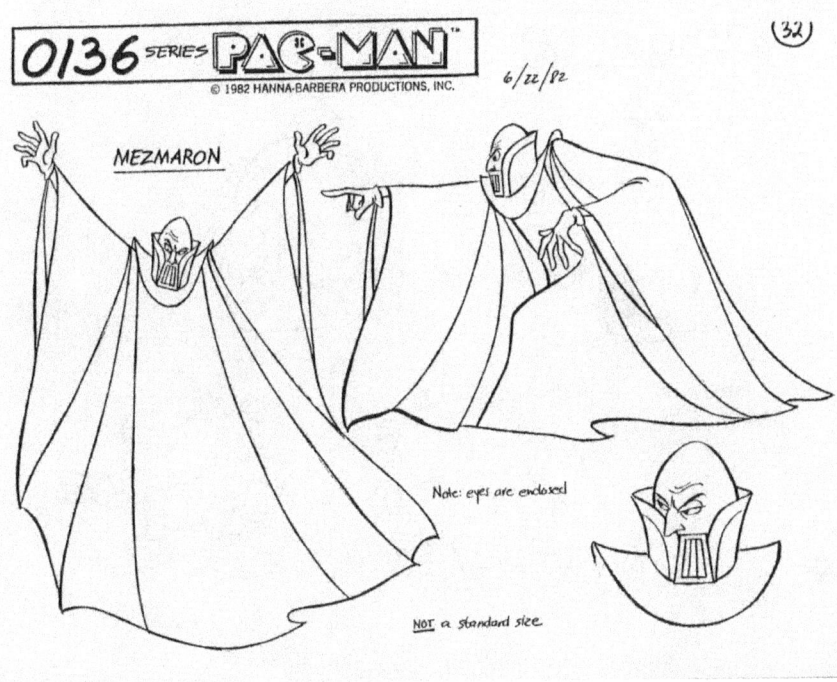

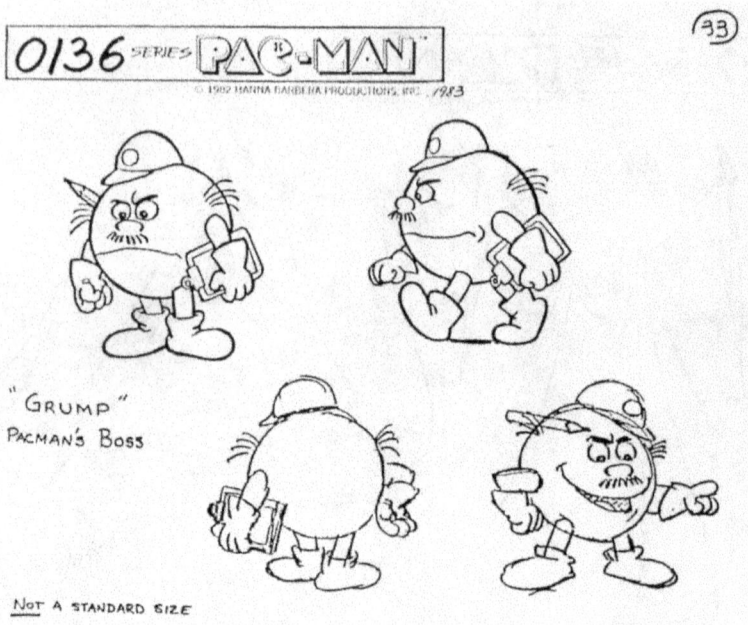

## Pac-Man Model Sheets 119

# Pac-Man Postscripts

## Pac-Man's 30th Anniversary

One of the highlights of Pac-Man's 30th anniversary in 2010 was a Google doodle that was created by Google doodler Ryan Germick. Germick said of the doodle, "I made sure to include Pac-Man's original game logic, graphics and sounds, bring back ghosts' individual personalities, and even recreate original bugs from this 1980s masterpiece. We also added a little Easter egg; if you throw in another coin, Ms. Pac-Man joins the party and you can play together with

someone else (Pac-Man is controlled with arrow keys or by clicking on the maze, Ms. Pac-Man using the W-A-S-D keys)."

## The Comic-Con Museum Character Hall of Fame

The Pac-Man character was inducted into the Comic-Con Museum Character Hall of Fame on December 17, 2020. There was a bit of controversy over this decision as some argued that a video game character isn't a comic book character, but the Comic-Con Museum maintains that they want to honor

Toru Iwatani in 2020

characters that have dominated and permeated nearly every aspect of popular culture, not just comic books.

On the day of the celebration, they told the story of Pac-Man and explored his past, present and future. Pac-Man creator Toru Iwatani celebrated Pac-Man's accomplishments to date and he gave the inside scoop as to what Pac-Man would be doing next.

There was also a performance by Ken Ishii, Japanese DJ, techno artist, composer, producer and originator of his new theme song called 'Join the Pac'.

Due to the pandemic of 2020, the entire celebration was shown on the Comic-Con Museum YouTube Channel.

## Pizza Hut Salute for Pac-Man's 40th Anniversary

Pizza Hut restaurant celebrated Pac-Man's 40th anniversary in the USA in 2020 and 2021 with a series of commercials starring comic actor Chris Robinson, who is shown eating a slice while playing the classic arcade game in a table version. To make the point more clear, the décor of his Pizza Hut harks back to what a Pizza Hut looked like during the late 1970s and early 1980s. The ad promotes the $10 Tastemaker pizza, but more than just pizza the outer cardboard box container has Pac-Man graphics on the lid. The box lid isn't just a design, it's also a game that can be played.

According to Yutaka Fuse, Head of Licensing and Branding at Bandai Namco Entertainment, Inc., "Pac-Man's design and creation was inspired by the shape of a pizza with a slice taken out of it."

While drawing up ideas for a game based around food, Iwatani grabbed a slice of pizza from a box and had an epiphany: The remaining pizza slices formed Pac-Man's shape, and the rest was history (or so the story goes, according to Iwatani).

Robinson said he had Pizza Hut memories. "Growing up in the 80s, mine was going into Pizza Hut and devouring those little Pac-Man dots just like I did my pizza. Those arcade games in the restaurant – there was nothing better as a kid."

**ABOUT THE AUTHOR:** *Mark Arnold was born in San Jose, and grew up in Saratoga, California. He is a comic book and animation historian, and has had many articles published in various publications. He has published books on TTV (Underdog, Tennessee Tuxedo),* Cracked *magazine, The Beatles, Walt Disney Productions, DFE (Pink Panther), Dennis the Menace, Alvin and The Chipmunks and The Monkees. He is currently working on a book about MAD magazine. He has also produced and recorded DVD commentaries for Shout! Factory and Kino Lorber and hosts his own Fun Ideas Podcast. He currently resides in Springfield, Oregon.*

# Index

*A Team, The* - 56
Abbott and Costello - 6
*Abbott and Costello Cartoon Show, The* - 6
Abbott, Bud - 6
ABC - 5-14, 30-35, 41
*ABC Afterschool Specials, The* - 9, 12
*ABC Saturday Morning Pac Preview Party, The* - 33
*ABC Saturday Superstar Movie, The* - 9, 49
*ABC Weekend Specials* - 12, 45, 47, 49, 52, 54, 56
"Abominable Pac-Man, The" - 76-77
Academy Awards (Oscars) - 3, 44
ACT - Action for Children's Television - 7
*Adam-12* - 41, 50
*Addams Family, The* - 10, 41, 50, 55, 57
*Adventure Time* - 47
*Adventures of Buckaroo Bonzai, The* - 20
*Adventures of Don Coyote and Sancho Panda, The* - 13, 44-45, 49-50
*Adventures of Gulliver, The* - 7
*Adventures of Ozzie and Harriet, The* - 57
*Adventures of Robin Hoodnik, The* - 9
*Adventures of Superboy, The* - 57
*Adventures of the Gummi Bears, The* - 47-48, 50, 54, 57
Air Programs International - 10
*Airwolf* - 56
*Aladdin* - 49, 54
*Alan Hamel Show, The* - 52
*Alan Thicke Show, The* - 52
Alcorn, Allan - 16
*Alfred Hitchcock Presents* - 45-46, 50-51
*Alice* - 43

*Alice in Wonderland* - 6, 55
*All in the Family* - 44, 51
*All-New Dennis the Menace, The* - 45, 47
*All New Popeye Hour, The* - 11, 50, 55, 57
*All-New Super Friends Hour, The* - 10
*All That Glitters* - 47
Allwine, Wayne - 43
*Alvin and the Chipmunks* - 48, 52, 54, 57
*Amazing Bunjee Venture, The* - 12
*Amazing Chan and the Chan Clan, The* - 9, 50, 57
Amazon Prime - 32
*America vs. the World* - 14
American International Pictures - 6
*American Tail, An* - 45
*Amigo and Friends* - 11
Ampex - 16
*Andy Griffith Show, The* - 55, 57
*Andy Williams Show, The* - 55
*Angry Beavers* - 55
*Animaniacs* - 45, 47, 49, 54, 56
*Ann Sothern Show, The* - 41, 45-46
*Annie Hall* - 53
Apex - 32
Apple Computers - 16
*Aqua Teen Hunger Force* - 14
Aquaman - 53
*Arabian Knights* - 7
Arad Productions - 32
Arby's - 29
*Arcade* - 25
*Archie Bunker's Place* - 46
Archie Comics - 8
*Arliss* - 54

Arnaz, Desi - 4
"Around the World in 80 Chomps" - 92
*Around the World in 80 Days* - 57
*Around the World in 79 Days* - 7
*Art of Hanna-Barbera: Fifty Years of Creativity, The* - 1
Asteroids - 1, 16-17
*Astro and the Space Mutts* - 7
Atari - 16-18, 21, 24, 28
Atom Ant - 6
*Atom Ant/Secret Squirrel Show, The* - 6, 57
*Attack of the Killer Tomatoes* - 45, 47
*Augie Doggie and Doggie Daddy* - 5
Autocat - 41
*Avatar: The Last Airbender* - 45, 54
Avery, Tex - 12

*B.B. Beegle Show, The* - 14
Baba Louie - 5
Baby Gonzo - 43
Baby Pac-Man - 24
"Backpackin' Packy" - 76
"Bad Case of the Chomps, A" - 80-81
*Baggy Pants and the Nitwits* - 56
*Bailey's Comets* - 49
Ball, Lucille - 4
Bally Midway - 17, 41
Bamm-Bamm Rubble - 5
*Banacek* - 41
*Banana Splits Movie* - 14
Banana Splits, The - 7-8
*Banana Splits, The* - 10, 49
*Banana Splits Adventure Hour, The* - 7
*Banana Splits in Hocus Pocus Park, The* - 9
*Bananas* - 25
Bandai Namco Entertainment - 21, 23-24, 32, 123
*Barkleys, The* - 52, 55
*Barney Miller* - 46
Barbera, Joseph (Joe) - 1, 3-4, 12, 14
*Baretta* - 43
Barney Rubble - 5, 11
*Barnyard Commandos* - 50, 54
Barton, Matt - 17
*Batman* - 45-46, 49-50, 54
*Batman Beyond* - 49
*Battle of the Planets* - 57
*Baxter!* - 9
Baxter, Les - 5
*Baywatch* - 41, 51

*Beach Girls, The* - 13
*Beasts are in the Streets, The* - 12
*Beauty and the Beast* - 51
Beck, Jerry - 1
*Becker* - 46
*Bedknobs and Broomsticks* - 50
Beegle Beagle - 41
*Belle Starr* - 12
*Ben 10* - 45
Benedict, Tony - 4, 6
*Benji, Zax & the Alien Prince* - 12
*Berenstain Bears, The* - 11, 54
Berzerk - 17
Betrayus - 32
Betty Rubble - 5
*Bewitched* - 6, 41, 55
*Big Love* - 54
Bigmouth - 50
*Biker Mice from Mars* - 45, 54
*Bill and Ted's Excellent Adventures* - 13, 54
Billboard - 18
*Biography* - 44
"Bionic Pac-Woman, The" - 77
*Bionic Six, The* - 45, 49
Birdie the Early Bird - 43
*Birdman and the Galaxy Trio* - 7
*Biskitts, The* - 12, 48, 51
*Black Beauty* - 8
*Blackstar* - 49
*Blast-Off Buzzard* - 10
Blinky - 31-32, 37, 46-47, 57, 65-95, 104-105, 111-112, 114, 121
*Blues Brothers, The* - 45
*Bob & Carol & Ted & Alice* - 43
*Bob Crane Show, The* - 46
*Bob Newhart Show, The* - 53, 55
*Bobby Darin Show, The* - 52
*Bobby Vinton Show, The* - 56
*Bobby's World* - 49, 52, 54, 57
*Bold and the Beautiful, The* - 54
*Bold Ones, The* - 44
*Bonanza* - 45
Bonkers - 45, 48-49, 54
*Book of Pooh. The* - 48
Boomerang - 14, 32
*Boys Next Door, The* - 20
*Boys' Ranch* - 50
*Brady Kids, The* - 50
*Brak Show, The* - 14
*Brave Little Toaster, The* - 45

*Bravestarr* - 48, 54
*Breezly and Sneezly* - 6
Brooklyn, New York - 42
Browsh, Jared Bahir - 1
Buckner and Garcia - 18-19
Buckner, Jerry - 28
*Bud and Lou* - 55
*Buford and the Galloping Ghost* - 9, 49-50
*Bugaloos, The* - 55
*Bugs Bunny Show, The* - 55
Bumblebee - 48
*Bungle Brothers, The* - 12
Burger Time - 1
*Burke's Law* - 41, 45
Bushnell, Nolan - 16
*Busy Body, The* - 41
*Butch Cassidy* - 49
*Butch Cassidy and the Sundance Kids* - 9
Butt-ler - 32
*Buzz Lightyear* - 49

*C.H.O.M.P.S.* - 9
Cahuenga Blvd. - 5
Canadian Broadcasting Corporation - 17
Callaway, William - 53-54
*Camp Candy* - 54
*Cannonball Run II* - 55
*Can't Buy Me Love* - 20
Cantinflas - 11
Capp, Al - 11
*Capitol Critters* - 14, 45, 49, 55
Captain Banshee - 32
Captain Caveman - 3
*Captain Caveman and the Teen Angels* - 8, 47, 49, 52, 54, 57
*Captain Planet and the Planeteers* - 13, 45, 49
Carlin, George - 13
Carlisle, Jodi - 54
Carlton the Doorman - 52
*Carlton Your Doorman* - 53
*Caroline in the City* - 46
Cartoon Network - 14, 32
*Cartoon Planet* - 14
Casey, Bernie - 13
*Casper and the Angels* - 11, 52
Casper the Friendly Ghost - 11, 22
*Cast of Friends, A* - 1
*CatDog* - 49
*Cattanooga Cats, The* - 7, 41, 54

*Cave Kids* - 14, 49
*CB Bears, The* - 10, 45, 47, 50, 52, 55, 57
CBS - 4, 7-14, 31
*CBS Storybreak* - 11, 45
Centipede - 1
*Centuri* - 17
*Centurions* - 45
*Challenge of the GoBots* - 12, 48-49, 51, 54, 57
*Challenge of the Super Friends* - 10
Charlie Chaplin Studios - 4
*Charlotte's Web* - 9, 55
*Chasing Ghosts: Beyond the Arcade* - 20
*China Beach* - 56
*Chip 'n' Dale's Rescue Rangers* - 47-49
*Chips* - 41, 53
Chomp-Chomp - i, 15, 30, 32, 34-36, 48-49, 53, 66-96, 103
"Chomp-Out at the O.K. Corral" - 77-78
*Christmas Comes to Pac-Land* - 32, 35-37, 83-84
*Christmas Story, A* - 14
Chuck E. Cheese's Pizza Time Theatre - 16
*Chuck McCann Show, The* - 47
*Cinderfella* - 46
Cinematronics - 17
Clark, Dick - 33
*Climax!* - 51
*Cloak & Dagger* - 20
*Clue Club* - 9-10, 52, 55
Clyde - 24, 31-32, 44, 57, 65-95, 104-107, 121
CNN - 22
Cobra Commander - 56
*Cold Case* - 54
Collins, Christopher - 56
*Color of Money, The* - 20
Columbia Pictures - 4, 6
*Columbo* - 47
*Combat!* - 45
Comic-Con Museum Character Hall of Fame, The - 122
*Completely Mental Adventures of Ed Grimley, The* - 13, 49
Computer Bug - 32
"Computer Game" - 18
"Computer Packy" - 93
Computer Space - 16-17
*Computer Wore Tennis Shoes, The* - 49

Cookie Crisp - 50
Cookie Jarvis - 50
*Cool McCool* - 47
Cosby, Bill - 41
Costello, Lou - 6
Count Floyd - 13
*Count of Monte Cristo, The* - 8
Count Pacula - 32
*Cow and Chicken* - 14, 49, 55, 57
*Cowboys of Moo Mesa, The* - 45, 54
*Cracked* - 1
Crackle - 49
*Crazy Claws* - 12
*Crazy Comedy Concert, The* - 9
Crazy Otto - 24
*Criminal Minds* - 54
*Crusader Rabbit* - 4
*CSI* - 41
*CSI: Miami* - 54
Cullen, Peter - 48
Culp, Robert - 41-42
Cummings, Brian - 54
*Curb Your Enthusiasm* - 46
*Curious George* - 45, 49
*Curiosity Shop* - 43
Cyber-Fluffy - 32
Cyber-Mouse - 32
Cylindria - 32
Cyclops - 32
*Cyrano* - 9

Da Mob - 45
Dabney, Ted - 16
*Daisy-Head Mayzie* - 14, 45
*Danger Island* - 7
*Daniel Boone* - 8
*Danny Phantom* - 49
*Danny Thomas Show, The* - 44, 46, 55
Danny Vaincori - 32
*Daphne & Velma* - 14
*Darkwing Duck* - 41, 45-46, 49, 53-55, 57
Darrin Stephens - 6
*Dastardly and Muttley in Their Flying Machines* - 7
*David Frost Show, The* - 55
*Davy Crockett on the Mississippi* - 8
*Dawn of the Dead* - 20
"Day the Forest Disappeared, The" - 74
*Deadline* - 12

*Dean Martin Celebrity Roast, The* - 52
*Dean Martin Show, The* - 56
Dees, Rick - 52
Defender - 17
*Defenders of the Earth* - 54
*Dennis the Menace* - 46
DePatie-Freleng Enterprises - 9, 11
*Desperate Housewives* - 54
*Destination Gobi* - 50
Devil, The - 41
*Devlin* - 10
Dewey - 43
DeWitt, Joyce - 14
*Dexter's Laboratory* - 14, 49
DIC - 13
*Dick Van Dyke Show, The* - 41, 50, 55
*Diff'rent Strokes* - 10
Dig Dug - 1, 17
Dig'em Frog - 49
*Dinah!* - 56
*Dink the Little Dinosaur* - 13, 49, 54
Dinky - 32, 51-52, 84-95
*Dinky Dog* - 11, 49
Dino - 5
*Dino-Riders* - 48
*Dirty Dawg* - 12
"Disco Space Invaders" - 18
Disney - 41
Disney XD - 32
"Do the Donkey Kong" - 18
*Don Rickles Show, The* - 46
Donkey Kong - 1, 17, 31
Donkey Kong Junior - 17, 31
*Donna Reed Show, The* - 55
Donner, Richard - 7
*Doogie Howser, MD* - 56
Do-Ug - 32
Dr. A.H. Buttocks - 32
*Dr. Dolittle* - 50
"Dr. Jekyll and Mr. Pac-Man" - 91
*Dr. Kildare* - 45-46, 51, 55
Dr. Pacenstein Fluffy - 32
*Dracula: Dead and Loving In* - 47
Drag Race - 16
*Dragnet* - 46
*Dragon's Lair* - 17, 48
*Drak Pack* - 11, 47, 52, 54
*Drew Carey Show, The* - 53
*Droopy: Master Detective* - 11, 46-47, 49, 54-55, 57

*Duck Dodgers* - 49, 55
*Duckman* - 47, 54
*DuckTales* - 43, 45, 47-49, 54-56
*Dukes, The* -10, 44, 48, 54-57
*Dukes of Hazzard, The* - 10, 56
*Dumb and Dumber* - 13, 45, 49
*Dungeons & Dragons* - 48-49
DVD - 31-32, 82
*Dynomutt* - 50

*Easter Pac-Peep, The* - 32
Ed Norton - 5
*Eddie Bracken Show, The* - 57
Eeyore - 48
*Eight is Enough* - 53
Elimination - 16
*Elliptika* - 32
*Elves and the Shoemaker, The* - 13
*Emergency!* - 44, 50
*Emmy Awards, The* - 44
*Emperor's New Clothes, The* - 13
*Emperor's New School, The* - 49, 54
*Empty Nest* - 46
Engel, Georgia - 14
*ER* - 41
Eric Porter Studios - 10
Evil Knievel - 10
*Evil Spirits* - 55

*Fabulous Dr. Tweedy, The* - 57
Facebook - 1
*Fairly OddParents, The* - 55
*Fame* - 56
*Family* - 41
*Family Guy* - 49
*Family Ties* - 43
*Famous Classic Tales* - 8
*Fangface* - 49
*Fantastic Four, The* - 7-8, 11, 45, 47, 49, 55, 57
*Fantastic Max* - 13, 45, 47, 53-57
*Fantasy Island* - 56
*Far Out Space Nuts* - 47
*Farmer's Daughter, The* - 50
*Fast Times at Ridgemont High* - 20
*FBI, The* - 57
*Ferngully* - 45
*Ferris Bueller's Day Off* - 20
Filmation - 8-10

*Fish* - 46
*Fish Police* - 14, 45, 49
*Five Weeks in a Balloon* - 8
Flaherty, Joe - 13
*Flintstone Comedy Show, The* - 8, 49
*Flintstone Funnies, The* - 8
*Flintstone Kids, The* - 8, 12, 44, 49-50, 52, 55-56
*Flintstones, The* - 5-6, 8-10, 57
*Flintstones Comedy Hour, The* - 8, 43
*Flintstones in Viva Rock Vegas, The* - 9
*Fluppy Dogs* - 53
Fonz, The - 31, 33
*Fonz and the Happy Days Gang, The* - 10, 33, 45, 49
*Foofur* - 12, 44-45, 48-49, 54, 56
*Footloose* - 20
Formula K - 16
41 Entertainment - 32
Foster, Warren - 4
FOX - 11
Fraley, Pat - 54-55
France -12
*Frankenstein Jr. and the Impossibles* - 7
Frankenstein's monster - 7
*Freakazoid!* - 45, 49
Fred - 32
*Fred and Barney Meet the Thing* - 8
*Fred and Barney Meet the Shmoo* - 8, 47
Fred Calvert Productions - 9
Fred Flintstone - 3, 5, 11
*Fred Flintstone and Friends* - 8, 52
Freddie the Flute - 55
*Free Guy* - 20
Frogger - 1, 31
*Fun with Dick and Jane* - 53
*Funky Phantom, The* - 9, 57
Funny Stuff - 18
*Funny World of Fred and Bunni, The* - 13
*Funtastic World of Hanna-Barbera, The* - 11-12
*Further Adventures of SuperTed, The* - 12, 49-50, 55-56
Fuse, Yutaka - 123
*Futurama* - 49
Fuzbits - 32

*Gallant Heart, The* - 57
Galaxian - 17

*Galaxy Goof-Ups* - 9, 50, 57
*Galaxy High School* - 45, 55
*Galtar and the Golden Lance* - 12, 47, 54-55
Garfield - 53
*Garfield and Friends* - 45, 47, 49-50, 54-55
*Garfield Show, The* - 49-50
*Gargoyles* - 49, 55
*Gary Coleman Show, The* - 10, 52
*Gathering, The* - 12
*Gathering, Part 2, The* - 12
General Computer Corporation - 24
*General Electric Theater* - 44
General MIlls - 6
Genii - 90
"Genii of Pacdad, The" - 90
George Jetson - 3
Gerald McBoingboing - 4
Gerber, Joan - 55
Germick, Ryan - 121
*Get Along Gang, The* - 47, 49
*Get Christie Love!* - 56
*Get Smart* - 10, 57
*Ghost Busters, The* - 41
*Ghostbusters* - 48, 55
Ghosteroid - 32
*G.I. Joe* - 44, 47-49, 54-56
*Gidget Makes the Wrong Connection* - 9
*Girl Can't Help It, The* - 46
*Girl from U.N.C.L.E., The* - 44
*Glen Campbell Goodtime Hour, The* - 55
*Glo Friends, The* - 45, 53, 55
Glooky - 32
*Go Go Gophers* - 6
*GoBots* - 48
*GoBots: Battle of the Rock Lords* - 9
Godzilla - 11
*Godzilla Power Hour, The* - 11
*Going Bananas* - 12
*Goldbergs, The* - 20
*Golden Globe Awards, The* - 44
*Golden Palace, The* - 56
*Gomer Pyle, USMC* - 53
"Goo-Goo at the Zoo" - 81-82
*Goober and the Ghost Chasers* - 9
*Good Morning World* - 41
*Good, the Bad and Huckleberry Hound, The* - 13
*Good Times* - 50

*Goof Troop* - 49, 54-55
Google - 121
*Goonies, The* - 20
Gordon, Barry - 46
Gordon, Dan - 4
*Governor and J.J, The* - 43
*Grady* - 44
*Gran Trak* - 16
Grannie - 32
Grant, Max B. - 19
*Grapes of Wrath, The* - 50
*Gravedale High* - 13, 46, 55
Great American Broadcasting - 13
Great American Communications - 13
*Great Gazoo, The* - 5
*Great Gilly Hopkins, The* - 12
*Great Grape Ape Show, The* - 41, 50
"Great Pac-Quake, The" - 67-68
"Great Power Pellet Robbery, The" - 80
*Greatest Adventure: Stories from the Bible, The* - 13, 51
*Greatest American Hero, The* - 47
"Greatest Show in Pacland, The" - 88-89
*Gremlins* - 48
*Grim Adventures of Billy & Mandy, The* - 49, 54-55, 57
Grimace - 49-50
Grinder - 32
Grinder-Tron - 32
Grindette - 32
Grump - 118
*Guardians of the Galaxy* - 50
*Gulliver's Travels* - 8
*Guide for the Married Man, A* - 41
*Gun Fight* - 17
*Gunsmoke* - 44-45, 51, 53
*Gymnast, The* - 9

H.R. Pufnstuf - 50
*H.R. Pufnstuf* - 55
*Hagar the Horrible: Hagar Knows Best* - 14
Hal Seeger Productions - 9
Halloween - 32
*Hamburger: The Motion Picture* - 47
*Hands of a Stranger* - 46
*Hanna-Barbera: A History* - 1
*Hanna-Barbera Cartoons* - 1
Hanna-Barbera Enterprises - 1, 4-14, 25, 30-32, 41, 44, 66, 84
*Hanna-Barbera Happy Hour, The* - 11

*Hanna-Barbera New Cartoon Show, The* - 5
Hanna-Barbera Records - 5
*Hanna-Barbera Superstars 10* - 12-13
*Hanna-Barbera Treasury, The* - 1
*Hanna-Barbera's World of Super Adventure* - 7
Hanna, William (Bill) - 1-2, 4, 12, 14
*Happy Days* - 10, 31, 50, 52
*Happy Hooker Goes to Washington, The* - 43
"Happy Pacs-giving" - 1, 95
*Hardcase* - 12
*Harlem Globetrotters, The* - 8
*Harlem Globetrotters Meet Snow White, The* - 14
Harmon, Larry - 6
*Harry's Girls* - 45
*Harvey Birdman, Attorney at Law* - 14, 45, 49
Harvey Comics - 1, 11
*Have Gun, Will Travel* - 45
*Hawaiian Eye* - 45
*Hazel* - 45
*HBTV* - 12
*Heart is a Lonely Hunter, The* - 47
*Heathcliff* - 48
Heatter-Quigley Productions - 7, 11
*Heidi's Song* - 9, 48, 55
*Help! It's the Hair Bear Bunch* - 8, 50, 54-55, 57
*Hennesey* - 41, 55
*Herbie Rides Again* - 47
*Hercules* - 49
*Herculoids, The* - 3, 7
*Here Come the Brides* - 45
*Here's Lucy* - 56
"Here's Super-Pac" - 84-85
"Hey, Hey, Hey,,,It's P.J." - 34, 85
*Hey There, It's Yogi Bear* - 6
*Heyyy, It's the King!* - 10
Hickman, Darryl - 50-51
Hickman, Dwayne - 50
*Highway to Heaven* - 45
*Hill Street Blues* - 44
*Hillbilly Bears, The* - 6
*Histeria!* - 49
History of Computing Project, The - 16
"Hocus-Pocus Pac-Man" - 68-69
*Hokey Wolf* - 4
Hollywood, California - 4-5
*Hollywood Squares, The* - 7, 52, 55

Hong Kong - 41
*Hong Kong Phooey* - 10, 49-50, 57
Honey Smacks - 49
*Honeymooners, The* - 5
*Hoober-Bloob Highway, The* - 50
Hoppy the Hopparoo - 5
*Hot Dog!* - 25
*Hotel* - 56
*Houndcats, The* - 55-56
*House of Mouse* - 48-49, 57
*How to Frame a Figg* - 49
*How to Win at Pac-Man* - 27
*Huckleberry Hound Show, The* - 4-5, 8
*Hudson Brothers Razzle Dazzle Show, The* - 48
Huey - 43
*Hugefoot* - 32
*Hughleys, The* - 44, 46
*Hulk Hogan's Rock 'n' Wrestling* - 44, 54
*Human Comedy, The* - 50
*Human Giant* - 56
Hunt, Gordon - 41-42
Hutton, Danny - 5
*Hyperman* - 45

*I Am the Greatest: The Adventures of Muhammad Ali* - 55
*I Am Weasel* - 14, 49
*I Dream of Jeannie* - 10, 55
*I Love Lucy* - 4, 6, 57
*I Know That Voice* - 47
*I Spy* - 41
*I'm a Big Girl Now* - 46
*I'm Dickens, He's Fenster* - 41
*If It's Tuesday, It Must Be Belgium* - 41
*In Living Color* - 48
"Invasion of the Pac-Pups" - 73
*It Isn't Easy Being a Teenage Millionaire* - 9
Ideal Toys - 5
Inch High, Private Eye - 50
*Inch High, Private Eye* - 10, 57
*Incredible Hulk, The* - 46-47, 53, 55
Indy 4 - 16
*Informant. The* - 49
Ingels, Marty - 39, 41-42
*Inhumanoids* - 45, 54, 56
Inky - 31-32, 37, 45, 57, 65-95, 104-105, 109-110, 114, 121
*Insight* - 44
*Inspector Gadget* - 49, 56

*Invasion* - 47
*Iron Man* - 45, 47
*Iron Sheriff, The* - 51
Irwin, Stan - 6
Ishii, Ken - 123
Ito, Willie - 4
*It's a Mad Mad Mad Mad World* - 50
*It's the Wolf* - 7
Iwatani, Toru - 22-23, 122-124

*Jabberjaw* - 9, 46, 49-50, 52, 57
*Jack and the Beanstalk* - 7, 57
*Jack Benny Program, The* - 45-46, 55
*Jakers! The Adventures of Piggley Winks* - 45
*James Bond Jr.* - 45, 55
*Jana of the Jungle* - 11
Japan - 18, 21-22
Jean - 32
*Jeannie* - 10, 52, 57
*Jellystone!* - 14
*Jem* - 44, 54
*Jetsons Meet the Flintstones, The* - 13
*Jetsons, The* - 5, 8, 12, 31, 44, 46-50, 52-55, 57
*Jetsons: The Movie* - 9, 45
Jobs, Steve - 16
*Joey Bishop Show, The* - 41, 55
*John Davidson Show, The* - 52
*Johnny Bravo* - 14, 49
Johnson, Arte - 14, 55-56
"Join the Pac" - 123
*Jokebook* - 11, 50
Jomar Productions - 6
Jones, Shirley - 41-42
*Jonny Quest* - 5, 8, 57
*Jonny's Golden Quest* - 14
Josie - 57
*Josie and the Pussycats* - 8, 57
*Josie and the Pussycats in Outer Space* - 8
"Journey Into the Pac-Past" - 86-87
"Journey to the Center of Pacland" - 73-74
*Joysticks* - 20
*Judging Amy* - 54
Judy Jetson - 57
*Julia* - 57
*Jungle Cubs* - 49
*Jungle King* - 17
*Justice League Unlimited* - 56

*Karate Kid, The* - 20, 45
Kee Games - 16
Keenan, Joe - 16
Kellogg's - 4-5, 7
Kelly, Gene - 7
*Kid Super Power Hour with Shazam!, The* - 46
*Kidd Video* - 45
*Kim Possible* - 49
*King Kong* - 48
*King of Kong: A Fistful of Quarters, The* - 20
*King of the Hill* - 55, 57
Kingpin Obtuse - 32
Kirby, Paul - 56
*Kiss for Corliss, A* - 50
*KISS Meets the Phantom of the Park* - 12
*Kissyfur* - 44, 49-50, 55
*Kojak* - 56
*Kolchak: The Night Stalker* - 46
Konami -17
*Korg: 70,000 B.C.* - 10
*Koyaanisqatsi* - 20
*Krofft Supershow, The* - 50
*Kung Fu* - 10
*Kung Fu Panda* - 45
*Kwicky Koala Show, The* - 12, 48-50, 55

La Brea Avenue - 4
*LA Law* - 45-46
*Ladies Man, The* - 41
*Lady of the Press* - 57
*Lady Sings the Blues* - 43
*Ladybugs* - 47
*Lancelot Link* - 55
*Land of the Lost* - 10
Lantz, Walter - 12
*Laredo* - 50
Larry Harmon Productions - 6
*Last Frontier, The* - 12
*Last Halloween, The* - 14
*Last of the Curlews, The* - 9
*Last of the Mohicans, The* - 8
*Last Starfighter, The* - 20
Latta, Chris - 56
*Laurel and Hardy* - 6, 57
*Laverne & Shirley* - 10
*Laverne & Shirley in the Army* - 10, 33, 52
*Leave it to Beaver* - 46

*Legend of Korra, Blaze and the Monster Machines, The* - 45
*Legends of the Superheroes* - 12
*Leslie Uggams Show, The* - 53
*Lieutenant, The* - 45
*Lidsville* - 50, 55
*Life and Legend of Wyatt Earp, The* - 51
*Li'l Abner* - 8, 11
*Lilo & Stitch* - 49
*Linda Lovelace for President* - 41, 43, 47
*Lippy the Lion and Hardy Har Har* - 5
*Little Dracula* - 45
"Little Ghost Q-Taro" - 22
*Little House on the Prairie* - 47
*Little Mermaid, The* - 45, 49, 55
*Little Nemo* - 45
Little Rascals, The - 1, 31, 33
*Little Rascals, The* - 11, 31, 33, 48, 50, 52, 54
*Little Troll Prince, The* - 14
*Littles, The* - 49, 52, 55
Loguidice, Bob - 17
*Loopy De Loop* - 4
*Loretta Young Show, The* - 51
*Lost in Space* - 9, 55
*Lotsa Luck!* - 43
*Lucy Show, The* - 57
Louie - 43
Love, Alex - 4
*Love, American Style* - 8, 43, 46, 51, 53
*Love at First Bite* - 46, 55
*Love Boat, The* - 41, 45, 56
*Lucky Luke* - 12, 48, 54-55
Lurie, Allan - 44

MacGeorge, Jim - 6
*Mad* - 1, 25-26, 50
*Mad About You* - 54, 56
Madame Ghoulashi - 32
*Magic School Bus, The* - 49
Magilla Gorilla - 3
*Magilla Gorilla Show, The* - 5, 57
"Making Millions, 25 Cents at a Time" - 17
*Malcolm in the Middle* - 54
Mallory, Mike - 1
Maltese, Michael - 4
*Mama's Family* - 56
*Man Called Flintstone, The* - 6

*Man from U.N.C.L.E., The* - 45, 50
*Manhunt* - 41
*Mannix* - 46
*Many Loves of Dobie Gillis, The* - 45, 51
Mario - 17
*Married with Children* - 56
*Marsupilami* - 49
Martin Prince - 43
Marvel Comics - 7
Marvel Productions - 11-12
*Mary Tyler Moore Show, The* - 53
*Mask, The* - 45, 49, 55
Mass Media, Inc. - 21
Master Goo - 32
*Match Game, The* - 56
*Matty's Funday Funnies* - 55
Maude - 51
Mavis - 32
McCann, Chuck - 47
McDonald's - 43, 49-50
*McDonaldland Fun Times* - 26
*McHale's Navy* - 45, 55
McMahon, Ed - 14
McWhirter, Julie - 52
*Meatballs & Spaghetti* - 46, 48
*Medium* - 54
*Meet Corliss Archer* - 57
*Meet Me in St. Louis* - 50
Mega-Grinder - 32
*Men in Black* - 55, 57
*Men of Boys Town* - 50
*Merv Griffin Show, The* - 56
Mexico - 11-12
Mezmaron - 31-32, 43-44, 66-95, 114-117
MGM Studios - 3-4, 12, 14
Mickey Mouse - 43
*Micro Ventures* - 7
*Midnight Madness* - 20
*Midnight Patrol: Adventures in the Dream Zone* - 13, 44
Midway - 16-17, 21, 24
*Mighty Ducks, The* - 49
*Mighty Man and Yukk* - 48
*Mighty Mouse: The New Adventures* - 45
*Mike Douglas Show, The* - 52, 56
*Millionaire, The* - 51
Minkus, Barbara - 43
Minnie Mouse - 43

Missile Command - 17
*Mister T* - 48, 57
*Moby Dick and Mighty Mightor* - 7
Moe Szyslak - 56
*Monchichis* - 11-12, 48, 55
*Monchichis/Little Rascals/Richie Rich Show, The* - 11
*Monster in My Pocket: The Big Scream* - 12
Montgomery Burns - 56
Mooby - 32
Moondog - 32
Moranis, Rick - 13
*Mork & Mindy* - 10, 33
*Mork & Mindy/Laverne & Shirley/Fonz Hour* - 10, 33, 44, 49-50, 52, 54
Morris - 49
*Mortal Kombat* - 45
*Most Important Person, The* - 50
*Mother Goose and Grimm* - 45
*Mother, Juggs & Speed* - 43
*Motormouse and Autocat* - 7, 41
*Mr. Belvedere* - 56
*Mr. Bogus* - 45
Mr. Do - 17
Mr. Dome - 32
Mr. Magoo - 4
*Mr. Peabody & Sherman Show, The* - 54
Mr. Strictler - 32
Ms. Globular - 32
Ms. Pac-Man - 17, 23-24, 27, 30, 121
Mumbly - 11
Mummy Wizard - 32
*Munsters, The* - 50
*Munsters Today, The* - 41
*Muppet Babies* - 43, 48-49, 55
*Murder, She Wrote* - 41, 56
Muse, Kenneth - 4
Music, Lorenzo - 53
Muttley - 11
*My Favorite Martian* - 50
*My Life as a Teenage Robot* - 45
*My Life in Toons* - 1
*My Little Pony* - 48, 50, 54-55
*My Three Sons* - 45
*Mystery Island* - 10

Nakamura, Masaya - 24
Namco - 17, 21-24, 30-31
*Nanny, The* - 51

NBC - 6-13
Neander-Pac-Man - 75-76
"Neander-Pac-Man" - 75-76
Nether-World - 32
*Network* - 51
*Never Say Never Again* - 20
*New Adam12, The* - 41
*New Adventures of Captain Planet, The* - 13
*New Adventures of Huckleberry Finn, The* - 5, 57
*New Adventures of Jonny Quest, The* - 12, 48, 51
*New Adventures of Mighty Mouse and Heckle & Jeckle, The* - 49
*New Adventures of Winnie the Pooh, The* - 47-48
*New Batman Adventures, The* - 45
*New Breed, The* - 45
*New Dick Van Dyke Show, The* - 46
*New Fred and Barney Show, The* - 8, 57
*New Mike Hammer, The* - 56
*New Scooby and Scrappy-Doo Show, The* - 9, 44, 54
*New Scooby-Doo Movies, The* - 9, 49, 52, 55, 57
*New Scooby-Doo Mysteries, The* - 54
*New Shmoo, The* - 11, 49
*New Yogi Bear Show, The* - 9, 12, 44, 48, 54-55
*Night Court* - 54, 56
*Night Gallery* - 56
*Night of the Comet* - 20
"Nighty Nightmares" - 82-83
*Nightmares* - 20
Nintendo Entertainment System - 17, 31
North America - 18, 21-23
*Northwest Ranger* - 50
*Not with My Wife, You Don't* - 50
*Nova* - 44
*Now You See Him, Now You Don't* - 49
*NYPD Blue* - 46, 56

*Oddball Couple, The* - 55
O'Drool - 32
Optimus Prime - 48
"Old Pac-Man and the Sea, The" - 88
*Oliver and the Artful Dodger* - 9
"On and On" - 18

*Once Upon a Brothers Grimm* - 55
"Once Upon a Chomp" - 79
*Once Upon a Forest* - 9
*101 Dalmatians* - 49
Orville Pac - 87
*Our Gang* - 11, 31
*Out of Sight* - 50
*Over the Top* - 20
Owl - 56

P.J. a.k.a. Pac-Jr. - i, 1, 31, 50-51, 53, 84-95, 119
"P.J. Goes Pac-Hollywood" - 91
"Pac-a-Thon" - 89
Pac-Ape - 92-93
Pac-Baby - i, 30, 32, 34-38, 41, 43, 49, 53, 66-96, 101
"Pac-Baby Panic" - 69-70
Pac-beard - 87
Pac-Land - 30-32, 66-95
*Pac-Land* - 31
"Pac-Love-Boat, The" 79-80
Pac-Man - i, 1, 15, 17-18, 21-41, 53, 57, 65-99, 121-124
*Pac-Man* - 1, 11, 30-31, 33-38
*Pac-Man Album, The* - 19
*Pac-Man and his Ghostly Adventures* - 32
"Pac-Man at 40: The Eating Icon That Changed Gaming History" - 22
*Pac-Man Christmas Album, The* - 19
*Pac-Man Christmas Story, The* - 19
"Pac-Man Fever" - 18-19
*Pac-Man Fever* - 28
*Pac-Man Halloween Special, The* - 31, 34, 83
"Pac-Man in the Moon, The" - 71-72
*Pac-Man/Little Rascals/Richie Rich Show, The* - 1, 11, 31, 33, 66
*Pac-Man/Rubik, the Amazing Cube Hour, The* - 11, 84
*Pac-Man 2: The New Adventures* - 31
Pac-Man's 40th Anniversary - 123
Pac-Man's 30th Anniversary - 121
Pac-Mania - 18
Pac-Mania Bumper - 67-95
"Pac-Mummy, The" - 82
Pac-President - 66
Pac-Topus - 32
Pac Trash Truck - 120

"Pac Van Winkle" - 1, 94
Pac-World - 32
*Pac-World* - 32
Pacinator, The - 32
Packensack Packers - 85-86
Paclantis - 88
Pacuda Triangle - 88
Pacula - 70
"Pacula" - 31, 70, 83
*Paddington Bear* - 13
*Pandamonium* - 44, 52
*Parker Lewis Can't Lose* - 56
*Partners, The* - 41
*Partridge Family 2200 A.D.* - 10, 49, 52, 55
*Partridge Family, The* - 10, 49, 56
*Paul Lynde Show, The* - 49
*Paw Paws* - 12, 44, 49, 55
PC - 17
*Pebble and the Penguin, The* - 45
*Pebbles and Bamm-Bamm Show, The* - 8, 50
Pebbles Flintstone - 5, 43
Penelope Pitstop - 57
*People are Funny* - 57
Pepper Pac-Man - i, 1, 30, 32, 34-38, 41-43, 51, 53, 66-97, 100, 122
*Perils of Penelope Pitstop, The* - 7
Perry Mason - 51
*Pete and Gladys* - 41
*Peter Potamus Show, The* - 5, 57
*Petticoat Junction* - 57
*Phantom Rebel, The* - 12
*Phil Silvers Show, The* - 41, 57
*Phyllis Diller Show, The* - 41
*Piglet's Big Movie* - 48
*Pink Panther and Sons* - 11, 44, 56
*Pink Panther Laugh-and-a-Half, Hour and a Half Show, The* - 50
*Pink Panther Show, The* - 45-46, 55-56
Pinky - 31-32, 37, 46-47, 57, 65-95, 104-105, 108, 114, 121
*Pinky and the Brain* - 45, 49
*Pirates of Dark Water, The* - 13, 45, 48-49, 52, 57
Pitfall Harry - 31
*Pixels* - 20
*Pixie and Dixie and Mr. Jinks* - 4
Pizza Hut - 123-124

*Plastic Man Comedy/Adventure Show, The* - 47, 50, 52
Playback - 18
*Playboy Video Playmate Calendar, The* - 44
Player One - 18
*Please Don't Eat the Daisies* - 57
*Pole Position* - 17, 44, 51, 54, 56
*Police Story* - 41
Pong - 16-18
*Pooh's Grand Adventure* - 48
*Pooh's Heffalump Movie* - 48
Popeye - 11
*Popeye and Son* - 11, 44
*Posse Impossible* - 10
*Pound Puppies* - 12, 47-50, 53-55
Power Forest - 66-95
Power-Pellet Pickers - 85-86
Power Pellets - 31, 66-95
*Powerpuff Girls, The* - 14, 47, 49
*Practice, The* - 46
*Precious Pupp* - 6
President Stratos Spheros - 32
"Presidential Pac-Nappers" - 66-67
*President's Analyst, The* - 55
*Press Your Luck* - 50
Pretenders, The - 18
Pretty Boy Pac - 87-88
Prima, Louis - 5
*Prince Valiant* - 45, 54
*Prisoner of Zenda, The* - 50
Professor Pointy Brains - 32
*ProStars* - 45, 54-55
*Pruitts of Southampton, The* - 55
*Psycho II* - 20
*Psycho III* - 20
*Puberty Blues* - 20
"Public Pac-Enemy No. 1" - 1, 87-88
Puckman - 22
*Punkin' Puss and Mushmouse* - 5
*Punky Brewster* - 44
*Pup Named Scooby-Doo, A* - 13, 44, 46-47, 51
*Puppy's New Adventures* - 9, 33, 48, 57
"Puss Gets the Boot" - 3
*Puss in Boots* - 13

Q*Bert - 31
*Quack Pack* - 45, 49, 54-55
Quadropong - 16

*Quick Draw McGraw Show, The* - 5
Quiz Show - 16

*Rabbit Test* - 53
*Rainbow Brite* - 48, 55, 57
*Rainbow Brite and the Star Stealer* - 48
*Ralph Breaks the Internet* - 20
*Rambo* - 45, 48-50
Rankin/Bass - 9
*Rapunzel* - 13
*Raw Toonage* - 55
*Rawhide* - 51
*Ready Player One* - 20
Reagan, President Ronald - 18
*Real Adventures of Jonny Quest, The* - 14, 49
*Real Ghostbusters, The* - 45, 48-49, 53-54, 56
Rebound - 16
*Recess* - 49
Reddy - 4
Reeves, Keanu - 13
*Return of the Bunjee, The* - 12
*Return to Eden* - 12
*Rhoda* - 43, 53
Rice Krispies - 49
*Rich Little Show, The* - 52
Richie Rich - 1, 11, 31, 33
Richie Rich - 11-12, 31, 33, 44-45, 47, 49, 55-56
*Richie Rich/Scooby-Doo Show, The* - 9, 11, 31, 49, 54-56
*Ricochet Rabbit and Droop-a-Long* - 5
Right Guard - 47
RKO General - 6
Roach, Hal - 31
*Road Rovers* - 49
*Robin Hood: Men in Tights* - 47
Robinson, Chris - 123-124
*Robonic Stooges, The* - 10, 49
*Robot Chicken* - 49, 54
*Rock Odyssey* - 14
*Rockford Files, The* - 47
*Rockin' with Judy Jetson* - 13, 48
*Rocky III* - 20
*Roger Ramjet* - 55
*Roman Holidays, The* - 8, 57
*Rookies, The* - 41, 56
*Rosanne* - 56

Ross, Neil - 44- 45
Rotunda - 32
Round Deer - 32
*Route 66* - 45
*Rowan and Martin's Laugh-In* - 55
*Rubik, the Amazing Cube* - 31, 44, 57
Ruby-Spears - 9-11, 13-14, 31
*Rude Dog and the Dweebs* - 48
Rudolph - 83-84
Ruff - 4
*Ruff and Reddy Show, The* - 4
*Rugrats* - 53-54
*Rumpelstiltskin* - 13
*Runaways, The* - 9

Samantha Stephens - 6
*Sampson and Goliath* - 6
*Sanford* - 44
*Santa Barbara* - 47
Santa Claus - 32, 35, 83-84
Santa Pac - 32
Saturday morning TV - 7, 10, 30, 33
*Saturday Night Live* - 13
*Saturday Supercade* - 31, 48-49, 52, 55
Saunders, Jesse - 18
*Savage Dragon* - 45
*Scary Scooby Funnies* - 9
*Scoob!* - 14
*Scooby & Scrappy-Doo Puppy Hour, The* - 9, 48
*Scooby-Doo* - 10, 12, 14
*Scooby-Doo and Scrappy-Doo* - 9, 33, 47-48, 54-57
*Scooby-Doo and the Ghoul School* - 13
*Scooby-Doo and the Reluctant Werewolf* - 13
*Scooby-Doo/Dynomutt Hour, The* - 9, 49, 52, 55
*Scooby-Doo Meets the Boo Brothers* - 13
*Scooby-Doo 2: Monsters Unleashed* - 14
*Scooby-Doo, Where Are You?* - 8-9, 49
*Scooby's All-Star Laff-a-Lympics* - 9, 49
*Scooby's Mystery Funhouse* - 9
Scott, Art - 4
Scott, Jeffrey - 66-95
Scrappy-Doo - 50
Screen Actors Guild - 46
Screen Gems - 4
*Screwball Squirrel* - 11
*SCTV* - 13

*Sea Hunt* - 45
*Sealab 2020* - 8, 54
*Sealab 2021* - 14
Secret Files of the Spy Dogs, The - 45, 55
Secret Squirrel - 6
*Secret World of Og, The* - 12
*Sectaurs* - 45
Sega - 17
*Seinfeld* - 56
Selleck, Tom - 41
Sennett, Ted - 1
*Sergeant T.K. Yu* - 14
*Sesame Street* - 55
*7th Heaven* - 54
*Sgt. Bilko* - 4-5
*Shake, Rattle and Roll* - 10
*Shark's Paradise* - 12
*Sharky's Machine* - 50
Shaw!, Scott - 1
*Shazzan* - 7, 57
Sherman Brothers, The - 9
*Sherri* - 43
*Shirley & Marty: An Unlikely Love Story* - 41
*Shirt Tales* - 12, 56
Shmoo, The - 8, 11
*Shnookums and Meat Funny Cartoon Show, The* - 49
*Shootout in a One-Dog Town* - 12
Short, Martin - 13
Shostak, Stu - 2
Sidney, George - 4
*Silent Movie* - 47
*Silent Night, Holy Night* - 14
Silo, Susan - 45
*Simpsons, The* - 5, 14, 43, 49, 56
*Sinbad Jr. and his Magic Belt* - 6
Sir Chomps-a-Lot - 74-75
"Sir Chomps-a-Lot" - 74-75
Sir Cumferance - 32
*Skatebirds, The* - 10, 50, 52
*Skedaddle* - 12
Skeebo - 32
*Sky Commanders* - 12
Smith, Hal - 56
*Smothers Brothers Comedy Hour, The* - 48, 53
*Smothers Brothers Show, The* - 46
*Smurfs, The* - 11-12, 44-50, 52, 54-57

*Snagglepuss* - 5
SNK - 17
*Snooper and Blabber* - 5
*Snorks* - 12, 46-49, 54-56
*Something Wild* - 20
*Sonic the Hedgehog* - 49, 55
*Sonny and Cher Comedy Hour, The* - 48
*Sonny Comedy Revue, The* - 48
Sour Puss - i, 15, 30, 32, 34-36, 47-48, 53, 66-96, 102
Southern Star - 11
"Southpaw Packy" - 69
*Southwest Passage, The* - 50
Space Ace - 17
*Space Cats* - 46, 50, 55
*Space Ghost and Dino Boy* - 7, 57
*Space Ghost Coast to Coast* - 14
"Space Invader" - 18
Space Invaders - 1, 16-18, 20
"Space Invaders" - 18
Space Invaders Tournament, The - 18
*Space Kidettes, The* - 6, 57
*Space Stars* - 7, 44, 47, 49-51
*Space Stars Finale* - 7
*Spacecats* - 45
Spacewar! - 16
Specter - 32
*Speed Buggy* - 9, 57
Spheria Suprema - 32
*Spider-Man* - 44, 48, 54
*Spider-Man and his Amazing Friends* - 44, 48-49, 54-57
Spike - 16
Spiraltron - 32
*Spirit is Willing, The* - 46
*SpongeBob SquarePants* - 49
*Spooktacular New Adventures of Casper, The* - 49, 54-55
*Sport Billy* - 49
Spring Break - 20
Sprint - 16
*Squiddly Diddly* - 6
St. Elsewhere - 44
Star Blazers - 56
Star Fairies - 14
*Star Trek: Deep Space Nine* - 46, 56
*Star Trek: The Next Generation* - 56
*Star Trek: Voyager* - 46
*Star Wars* - 17, 45
Starchild - 32

Starscream - 56
*Starsky and Hutch* - 47
*Steadfast Tin Soldier, The* - 13
Stevens, Chris Erik - 56
Stewart, Mike - 28
Stojka, Andre - 56-57
*Stone Fox* - 12
*Stranger Things* - 20
Strawberry Shortcake - 43
*Strongest Man in the World, The* - 50
*Stu's Show* - 2
Sue - 24, 31-32, 37, 44-45, 51, 57, 65-95, 104-105, 113-114, 121
Sunny - 32
*Super Dave* - 45
*Super Friends* - 10, 47, 49, 52-53, 55
*Super Friends: The Legendary Super Powers Hour* - 10
"Super Ghosts" - 71
*Super Globetrotters, The* - 8, 49-50, 57
Super-Pac - i, 1, 31, 52-53, 84-95
"Super-Pac-Bowl, The" 85-86
Super Pac-Man - 24-26. 30
"Super-Pac vs. Pac-Ape" - 92-93
*Super Powers Team: Galactic Guardians, The* - 10
*Super Secret Secret Squirrel* - 13
*Super 6, The* - 55-56
Superbug - 16
Superman - 45-46, 49, 54, 56-57
*Superman: The Movie* - 7
*Superstore* - 54
*Supertrain* - 46
*SWAT Kats: The Radical Squadron* - 13, 45-46, 49, 56-57
*Sylvester & Tweety Mysteries* - 45, 49, 56

*Tabitha and Adam and the Clown Family* - 9
Taft Broadcasting - 6, 13
*Taggart's Treasure* - 13
Taito - 17
*Take This Job and Shove It* - 20
*Tales of Terror* - 50
*Tales of Wells Fargo* - 51
*TaleSpin* - 45, 47-49, 53-55
Tank - 16
*Tarzan* - 46
*Tattletales* - 56
*Taxi* - 53

Taylor, Russi - 43
TBS - 13
*Teen Force* - 7
*Teen Wolf* - 11
*Teenage Mutant Ninja Turtles* - 46, 48, 54-55
Televisa - 12
*Tempest* - 1, 17
Tengen - 31
*Tennessee Tuxedo* - 6
*Terminator, The* - 20
Terri - 43
*Texan, The* - 44
*That Girl* - 43, 53
*That 70s Show* - 54
*These Are the Days* - 10, 50, 55, 57
*They Went Thata-Way and That-a-Way* - 47
*Thing, The* - 8
*Third Day, The* - 55
*13 Ghosts of Scooby-Doo, The* - 9
*This is America, Charlie Brown* - 49, 56
*Thousand Clowns, A* - 46
Three Dog Night - 5
*Three Musketeers, The* - 7-8
*Three's a Crowd* - 48
*Three's Company* - 46
*Thrill of it All, The* - 50
*Thriller* - 46
*Thumbelina* - 13, 45
*Thundarr the Barbarian* - 47, 52, 57
*Tick, The* - 45, 47, 55
*Tigger Movie, The* - 48
*Time* - 26
*Time for Timer* - 50
Time Warner - 14
*Timeless Tales from Hallmark* - 13
Timer - 50
*Timon and Pumbaa* - 49, 55
*Tingler, The* - 51
*Tiny Toon Adventures* - 49, 55
*Tiny Tree, The* - 57
Tip - 32
Tokyo, Japan - 21
Tom & Jerry - 3-4, 10-11, 22
*Tom & Jerry* - 14
*Tom & Jerry Comedy Show, The* - 49
*Tom & Jerry/Grape Ape Show, The* - 10, 41
*Tom & Jerry/Grape Ape/Mumbly Show, The* - 10
*Tom & Jerry Kids* - 11, 44-49, 54-57

*Tom & Jerry/Mumbly Show, The* - 10
*Tom & Jerry Show, The* - 45, 49-50
*Tom & Jerry: Spy Quest* - 14
*Tom & Jerry: The Movie* - 14
*Top Cat* - 5
*Top Cat Begins* - 14
*Top Cat: The Movie* - 14
*Top Cat and the Beverly Hills Cats* - 13
Total TeleVision productions - 6
*Touché Turtle and Dum-Dum* - 5
*Town Santa Forgot, The* - 14
*Toxic Crusaders* - 45, 47
*Toy, The* - 20
*Transformers, The* - 12, 44-45, 48-49, 56
*Trapper John, MD* - 56
Travalena, Fred - 14
"Trick or Chomp" - 31, 70-71, 83
*Trollkins* - 12, 49-50, 54
*TRON* - 20
*TRON: Legacy* - 20
*Trouble with Girls, The* - 49
"Turkey in the Straw" - 31
Turner Broadcasting System - 14
Turner Feature Animation - 9
Turner, Ted - 14
Tutenpac-man - 86-87
*TV Bloopers & Practical Jokes* - 52
*20,000 Leagues Under the Sea* - 8
*Twilight Zone, The* - 44, 50, 55
Twin Racer - 16
*Twisted Tales of Felix the Cat, The* - 45, 47, 55
*2 Stupid Dogs* - 13, 54

*Ugly Betty* - 54
*Ugly Duckling, The* - 13
Ultra Tank - 16
*Ultraman: The Adventure Begins* - 9
*Uncle Croc's Block* - 50
Uncle Vic - 18
*Undercover Elephant* - 10
United States of America - 23
Universal Pictures - 41
*Untouchables, The* - 51
UPA - 4
USA Cartoon Express - 32
Üter - 43

*Valentine's Day* - 45
*Valley of the Dinosaurs* - 10, 49

*Velveteen Rabbit, The* - 12
VHS - 32
"Video Game Stars: Pac-Man" - 17
*Video Games* - 27
*Vidiot* - 27
Vinci, Carlo - 4
*Vintage Games* - 17
*Visionaries* - 45, 56
*Voltron* - 44, 48, 50
*Voyagers!* - 44

*Wacko* - 52
*Wacky Races* - 7, 11, 57
*Wagon Train* - 45
*Wait Till Your Father Gets Home* - 8, 55
*Wake, Rattle and Roll* - 13, 57
Waldo, Janet - 57
*Walker, Texas Ranger* - 41, 56
*Wally Gator* - 5
Walt Disney Productions - 9
*Waltons, The* - 10, 50
*WarGames* - 20
Warner Archives - 31, 36-37
Warner Bros. Animation - 14
Warner Communications - 16
*Waynehead* - 49
Webigail Vanderquack - 43
Weinrib, Lennie - 50
Welker, Frank - 49-50
*What a Cartoon!* - 14, 47
*Wheelie and the Chopper Bunch* - 10, 49-50
*Where's Huddles?* - 8
*Where's Waldo?* - 45, 49, 55
Wilbur Pac - 87
*Wild and the Innocent, The* - 55
*Wild Thornberrys, The* - 49, 54
*Wild Wild West, The* - 45, 53
*Wildfire* - 13, 44, 51, 57
Williams - 17
Williams, Robin - 42
Wilma Flintstone - 5
Wilson, Rita - 13
Winkler, Henry - 33
*Winnie the Pooh* - 48, 56
*Winsome Witch* - 6
Winter, Alex - 13

Wolf, Mark J.P. - 17
*Wolfman Jack Show, The* - 48
Wolper Productions - 6
*Wonder Wheels* - 10
*Wonderbug* - 49
*Woody Woodpecker* - 55
*Woofer and Wimper* - 10
*World: Color it Happy, The* - 13
*World's Greatest Super Friends, The* - 10
Wozniak, Steve - 16
*Wreck-It Ralph* - 20
*Wuzzles, The* - 54
Wynn, Ed - 5

*Xiaolin Showdown* - 45

*Yakky Doodle and Chopper* - 5
Yellow Magic Orchestra (YMO) - 18
Yen - 18
*Yes Virginia, There is a Santa Claus* - 45
*Yippee, Yappee and Yahooey* - 6
*Yo Yogi!* - 9, 13, 45, 55-56
*Yogi and the Invasion of the Space Bears* - 13, 48
Yogi Bear - 9
*Yogi Bear* - 4, 8, 10, 14
*Yogi Bear and the Magical Flight of the Spruce Goose* - 13
*Yogi Bear Show, The* - 5, 8
*Yogi the Easter Bear* - 14
*Yogi's Ark Lark* - 9
*Yogi's Gang* - 9, 50
*Yogi's Great Escape* - 13, 54
*Yogi's Space Race* - 9, 49-50
*Yogi's Treasure Hunt* - 9, 12, 50, 57
*You Again?* - 43
*You're a Good Man, Charlie Brown* - 43
*Young Love* - 57
*Young Robin Hood* - 13
*Young Sampson* - 6
YouTube - 123
*Yum Yums: The Day Things Went Sour, The* - 14
Yune, Johnny - 14

Zac - 32
*Zorro* - 45

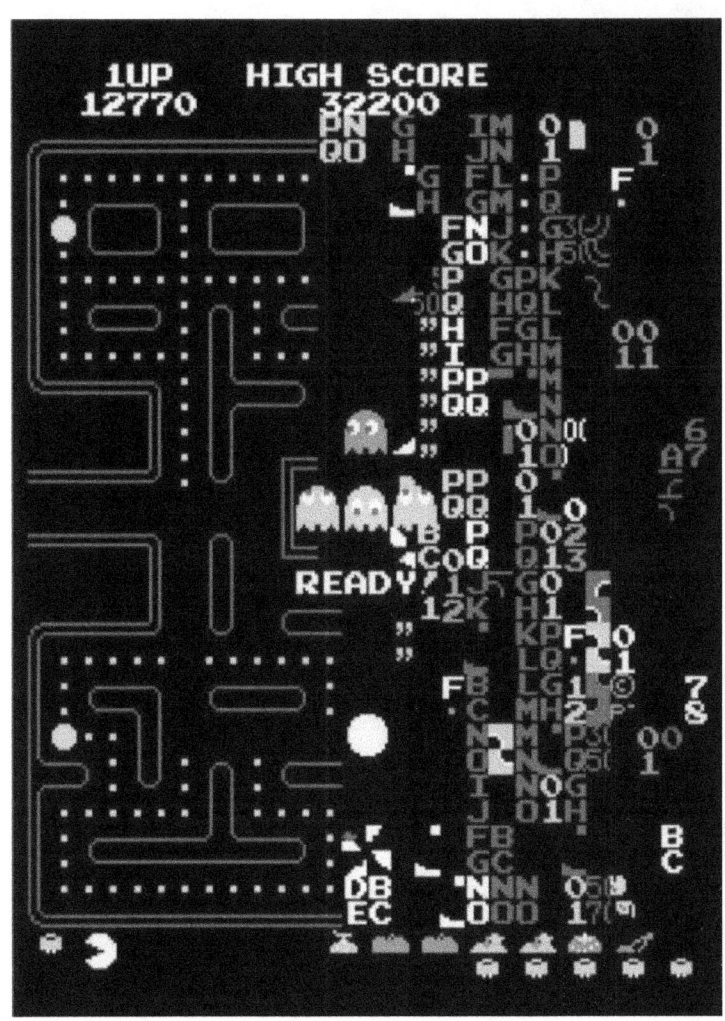

**GAME OVER**

**COMING SOON: HANNA-BARBERA'S PONG**

www.ingramcontent.com/pod-product-compliance
Lightning Source LLC
Chambersburg PA
CBHW071436160426
13195CB00013B/1922